Gifted and Talented Children 4–11

Can you recognize and tell the difference between gifted and talented children? Do you know how to provide the support they need?

Responding directly to current thinking in education, this book raises practitioners' expectations, and provides activities to help you identify children in your class as gifted and talented.

Christine Macintyre addresses the nature/nurture debate in relation to gifted and talented children, and discusses related topics such as the norms of development and domains of learning.

Essential reading for all primary teachers and teaching assistants, this fascinating book is full of practical suggestions enabling you to:

- recognise the innate nature of giftedness;
- provide the teaching required for talent to emerge;
- understand the experiences of gifted and talented children;
- develop activities to challenge and encourage your gifted and talented children to widen their repertoire of skills and abilities.

A chapter on neurological development is included to confront questions such as 'what is it that enables children to do well?', and even 'is there a gene for genius?' Contrasting and conflicting answers are shared and debated.

Finally, the issue of gifted and talented children with a learning difference/disability is raised and examples are given of how this ASD (asynchronous development) can hinder the recognition of gifts and talents in these children.

Christine Macintyre is a fellow of the University of Edinburgh.

Gifted and Talented Children 4–11

Understanding and supporting
their development

Christine Macintyre

Routledge
Taylor & Francis Group

LONDON AND NEW YORK

First published 2008
by Routledge
2 Park Square, Milton Park, Abingdon, Oxon OX14 4RN

Simultaneously published in the USA and Canada
by Routledge
270 Madison Avenue, New York, NY 10016

Routledge is an imprint of the Taylor & Francis Group, an informa business

© 2008 Christine Macintyre

Typeset in Garamond by
HWA Text and Data Management, Tunbridge Wells
Printed and bound in Great Britain by
Bell & Bain Ltd., Glasgow, Lanarkshire

British Library Cataloguing in Publication Data
A catalogue record for this book is available from the British Library

Library of Congress Cataloging-in-Publication Data
Macintyre, Christine, 1938–
Gifted and talented children 4–11 : understanding and supporting their
development / Christine Macintyre.
     p. cm.
  Includes bibliographical references and index.
  1. Gifted children–Education–Great Britain. I. Title.
  II. Title: Gifted and talented children four to eleven.
  LC3997.G7M33 2008
  371.95'72–dc22   2007045276

ISBN10: 0–415–46492–7 (pbk)
ISBN10: 0–203–92761–3 (ebk)

ISBN13: 978–0–415–46492–5 (pbk)
ISBN13: 978–0–203–92761–8 (ebk)

For Kirsten Duffus – a special child

Contents

Figures

Tables

Acknowledgements

There are many people who have contributed to this book and I should like to thank them all. Parents, teachers and the children themselves gave generously of their time and provided many insights into the complexities of identifying gifted and talented children while sharing ideas and strategies to support them. Many professionals relished the challenge of leaving ownership of learning with the children while finding ways to take them forward. Very often this needed some restructuring of the day to provide more time for the children to develop and evaluate their work and this was hard in the pressures of completing all that had to be done. However the children's enthusiasm was energetic and sustained because they were able to follow their particular interests, find new resources and accomplish things they had not attempted before. Often they surprised their teachers and themselves! These ideas were shared with all the children in the groups and so the learning of all the children was enhanced. The teachers also found that the children had raised their performance in line with their own raised expectations.

Thank you too for the expertise at Taylor and Francis. The professionals there have structured the many practical ideas, illustrations of children's work and theoretical stances into a book that is meant to help practitioners understand the varied aspirations and challenges that often arise in being gifted and talented with a learning difference or not. It is meant to encourage professionals to take a child-centred curriculum right through school. I hope it does.

Introduction
Discussing the issues

Let's listen to some people who really know what it's like to be 'gifted or talented' so that we can understand and empathise with their highs and lows. Adults set the scene with two quotations then different children explain how being gifted and/or talented feels for them!

First, Marland (1972) who gives an internationally recognised and agreed definition, explaining that:

> Gifted and talented children are those identified by professionally qualified persons who by virtue of outstanding abilities are capable of high performance.

While this is thought-provoking and makes us realise that experts in each field are needed to make such assessments, the mother of a gifted four-year-old makes us smile when she exclaims:

> They are children who do everything at the wrong time!

She reveals that raising a gifted and talented child breaks 'normal' expectations. It is not always easy!

Now listen to some children who explain what it's like to be different to the others in their class. They have all been identified as being gifted and talented (see Appendix 1 for criteria).

First Rachel, who is eight:

> I'm Rachel. At school I like being able to do things the others can't do but I don't like when I get called smarty pants or when the others won't play me at chess any more. School used to be a bit boring but now that my teacher knows that I'm really interested in the new planets I get time to do research and that is fascinating. The trouble is that no one else is and when I ask if they want to join me they come for a moment but then they go away and don't discuss things. I would love a friend to work with. The teacher doesn't have much time but she does mark my project or she sends me to show it to the special needs teacher. My Dad helps at home. We investigate astrophysics on the Internet and then I collate the material next day in school. I enjoy helping the wee ones with their work, but not all the time because that doesn't help me to learn more, does it?

So Rachel finds it hard to sustain social interactions and wants to limit her time as a 'helper', a role often ascribed to very able children, because she recognises that this reduces her time for personal study. She also highlights the challenges teachers face in providing both time and appropriate resources for able children.

Now Tim, who is ten:

> I'm Tim, and I'm exceptionally good at maths. I've always found sums easy. Even when I was three, Mum remembers me making puzzles for my toys. When I get asked to count, I see pictures of numbers in my head and they merge or pull apart to give the answer. My elder brother Garry has Down's syndrome and when he was learning his maths he used the Numicon system; that's

like dominoes with each number having its own picture. Maybe that's why I picked up maths easily. Of course my Dad lectures in maths at the University so he was pleased when I showed that I was interested in maths too. I can do square roots without a calculator and I'd rather have a page of equations than go out to play. At school I do my maths within a special group and I'll go to a Saturday class when I'm older. I like challenges like understanding how architects make measurements for bridges, things like that. The other kids call me the wizard. They don't mind my being top in maths because I'm hopeless at football and that's much more important to them!

Tim has prevented being isolated/resented/teased for his outstanding maths ability by almost trading off his poor football skills. His social skills have been successful in keeping him one of the crowd! He also recognises that his innate, probably inherited abilities have been boosted by his early exposure to a visual method of understanding patterns.

Jake, at only five, has already self-evaluated the implications of having developed (perhaps over-developed) altruism and empathy. He explains:

I think too much and get very sad because I can't help the children that go to the special school just along the road. I took them some toys and books but they couldn't even hold them. Why does God make some children have lives like that? My special friend is Marian and she smiles when I speak to her but she can't even feed herself or say when she is in pain. It makes me so unhappy for her and I wonder how my Mum and Dad would cope if it were me. Sometimes I can't work for thinking, I just want to cry.

How does one support such a hypersensitive child? Perhaps, after all, thinking too much is not the best way.

Ian at ten is much more confident. Interestingly he has ASD (asynchronous development, see Chapter 5). Listen to his story:

My name is Ian and I'm pleased it's a short name because I have severe dyslexia and writing things down can be a real pain. But that's OK because I just work out how to sort the computer or make models without reading the instructions. When my teacher said, 'You have to be able to read and write properly', I asked, 'Why is that? I am good with patterns and diagrams – I can manage perfectly well'. I am very creative, right brain dominant I think and I love solving problems. Some of the children in my class told me I was stupid because of my writing, so I challenged them to do the Rubik cube faster than me. That showed them. Anyway I use the computer now and that checks my spelling so as I have these other gifts, I wouldn't swap with them, would you?

Ian shows how a positive self-esteem is very necessary, even in a highly talented child and particularly those with ASD. His teacher had adhered to the strategy of promoting the gift while supporting the less able area and this had proved a successful strategy in Ian's case.

Sam at nine was less motivated by his talent. He tells his story:

My mother tells me I'm talented at athletics and yea I suppose I can run faster than anyone else in our gang so just to please her I went to the athletics ground to watch and then meet the relay team who were scouting for young talent. Actually, they dropped the baton and were last - how impressive was that? However I listened to Mum going on and on about how I could be an international athlete one day and I got quite interested. Then I found I had to get up to practise every morning before school even if it was raining! Not for me I said! No way! Forget it!

Sam highlights the problem of talented children who have the ability but lack the perseverance to fulfil their potential. Sam's parent's dreams are not going to be fulfilled – at least in the athletics sphere! Intrinsic motivation is essential if a long period of training is required!

And so the children, the most important people in this research, show that their gifts are wide and varied and that there can be downsides to having special abilities. This level of understanding is essential if teachers and other practitioners are to select comprehensive criteria to distinguish these children, an essential first move in providing a challenging appropriate and relevant curriculum.

Let's consider identifying gifted and talented children in the Nursery/Foundation stages now. Lacking experience, they may be less able to explain.

So who are the children who come into our early years' settings? They are a group of very young people of different ages (and remember that one year can mean one-third of a child's life span) and different developmental stages (some of the three-year-olds may be more able than the four-year-olds); different shapes, sizes, skin tones, intellectual abilities, social competences, movement skills, and emotional stability. They may have the expressive language to share their needs or difficulties making them known; they will have different dialects and different levels of understandings and acceptance of the nursery 'rules' that keep them all safe.

There are temperamental differences too, so that in any group there are confident children ready to take the lead; creative children who have innovative ways of solving problems; easy-going children who take life as it comes and children that are acutely anxious and who need a great deal of reassurance before they can settle and enjoy their time in school. There are slow-to-warm-up children and those that will not or cannot wait. The children have different family relationships with different levels of support. They have hugely varied home and out of school experiences and resources, opportunities to socialise with other children or only adults and they have different cultural and religious beliefs. Each one is unique (DES 2007; City of Edinburgh Council 2008). Is it any wonder that when all these children come together, practitioners wonder how they will be able to observe them all across all aspects of their development, identify those who are gifted and talented and develop curricular opportunities that take their developmental stage as a starting point yet offer learning challenges to enhance the learning of them all?

So what do practitioners do?

First, practitioners certainly make global assessments based on developmental milestones, but also based on listening to the children, observing what they do and recording the quality of their interactions. They also note what the children choose not to do, for this can mean a child has already self-assessed and decided to avoid experiences that could be difficult. Practitioners always acknowledge the effect of the children's previous experiences ; for example, if some children have no stairs at home they would probably climb using the step-together pattern longer than those who have stairs, or if some children arrive at school with friends then they could be expected to settle more quickly. Such observations allow practitioners to build a wide-ranging assessment profile for each child. Gradually they refine these first observations and plan learning opportunities based on their understanding of each child's developmental status, their preferences and their readiness for new challenges. Formally, through testing, or informally, through comparing children's performance to their peers in the setting, they consider these recordings against generally accepted norms of development (see Appendix 1). This practice is the same whether the children are gifted, talented, able, just 'average' or whether they have some impediment that means that their learning requires extra support. But as this book is concerned primarily with the children who would come into the gifted, talented and able group, and who would be expected to score 30 per cent higher than their peers (see Appendix 2 for lists of criteria) the focus will be on these children and the complex questions that have to be answered before the best practice can be assured. Questions such as:

- What is intelligence and how many children are likely to be gifted and talented in any group? (Introduction)
- Should children at this early age be given a label that sets them apart from others? Do the competences they display at three, four, and five years endure? (Introduction)
- What are the distinctions between gifted and talented children? (Chapter 1)

- Can children be gifted in one aspect and just ordinary in others, or do they have to be outstanding right across the board? (Chapter 1)
- Are the characteristics or traits of giftedness inherited i.e. is there a gene for genius or is a high level of achievement dependent on the quality of the environment? Is nature or nurture more important? (Chapters 2 and 3)
- Are the brains of gifted and talented children different? If so, what are the differences and how do these influence teaching (Chapters 2 and 3)
- What kinds of teaching input, i.e. activities and interactions, will challenge these children? How can practitioners fulfil the goals of the Early Years Foundation Stage (EYFS) and the Scottish Curriculum for Excellence in preparing input for these children? How do such activities prepare children to be innovative and creative thinkers? (Chapter 4)
- Is it possible to be gifted and have a learning difficulty? (Chapter 5)

These are important practical questions with underlying conceptual and philosophical issues that researchers are still debating. So should practitioners just wait till everyone agrees? Or given that research is based on unique children, will they ever agree? It is important that practitioners listen to the debate and understand the complexities that prevent easy resolutions. For the plethora of questions reveals that educating gifted and talented children is not easy. It requires a great deal of preparation, planning and even in-school debate about the identification of these children and ways to nurture them. And of course decisions are not only down to the school, for parents and carers are centrally involved too. All practitioners appreciate the importance of building positive relationships with parents because they have the most intimate knowledge of their children. They have the ultimate responsibility for them; they make the final decisions about what kind of education they should have and they have already taught them many things. And so it is only right that parents are intimately involved in deliberations that concern their child.

But what happens if parents insist their child is gifted and the practitioners do not agree? Or perhaps the practitioners put forward their assessments as evidence of the child's gifts and the parents don't want to know? Perhaps the parents are highly sceptical, doubting the practitioners' judgement, or maybe they are overjoyed and react by suggesting that they will give the child extra lessons at home? This idea in itself could be a source of conflict. Some parents, not recognising the learning that is implicit in the word 'play', might resent the early years' curriculum and urge practitioners to give more formal work. Or maybe the parents are bewildered and exhausted by their child's gifts and demands and just don't know how to cope, for bringing up a gifted child makes huge demands on time and resources. In many homes today neither of these may be readily available. What happens in these situations? Do the practitioners have to agree with the parents or adjust their practice to meet their views? In cases like these, how can positive relationships be sustained?

Or if the parents accept that they have a gifted or talented child but ask 'Well, what should we do now?' do the practitioners or the school have a strategy/policy in place? Is enhancement, enrichment or acceleration the best way for children in the early years? (See Chapters 1 and 4.) That is an important question, for assessment is of little use on its own; it must lead to a plan of action. Or should all children, especially gifted and talented ones, of any age be given more time to play? In play children have freedom; they can make choices and often pursue an idea to a level not envisaged by the teacher. They stay in charge of their project and find novel ways to work. This is not time wasting, in my view this is the core of education. Wordsworth in his ode 'Intimations of Immortality' claims that

> Heaven lies about us in our infancy!
> Shades of the prison-house begin to close
> Upon the growing Boy,

Could these in today's parlance be tests and ticks?

Some schools have been criticised for not paying enough attention to their gifted and talented pupils, often believing that they would be all right, their gifts would help them cope on their own. But educationalists now emphasise that ability must be recognised and nurtured at the earliest possible time. Some, for example Winner 2007, claim that 'it is never too early to begin' for if this doesn't happen, the critical window or learning time may be missed. She points out that at birth children 'have been listening for twelve weeks already' so they have the capacity to learn already in place. Furthermore, some gifted and talented children, once they develop self-knowledge at about three to four years, recognise they are different and hide their gifts and talents so that they appear the same as their friends. In both these scenarios, talents would be lost. Additionally some bright children can recognise their gifts but lack the motivation to make full use of their abilities. They have the aptitude but not the attitude, so it is important that they are stimulated to overcome this lethargy so that they may fulfil their potential too!

Practitioners often ask for guidance on the numbers of children they should expect to feature in their gifted and talented list. They report that they are confused by the terminology 'able, gifted and talented'. While some regions do not suggest specific numbers, the Gagné model (see Chapter 1) indicates that practitioners should nominate the top fifteen per cent of pupils in each ability domain.

But, while identifying different abilities in children, practitioners have to recognise how difficult it is to provide tests that give a comprehensive reading of a child's abilities, especially as even definitions of 'intelligence' have changed over the years.

Some pointers

- Some of the older IQ tests are limited in scope; they are too narrow to give a comprehensive picture of ability and despite huge efforts to make the items test ability rather than what has been learned, they can be culturally biased – they depend on opportunity and experience/ practice rather than innate potential. So they measure only a limited part of what might be called 'intelligence'. Children may be socially, emotionally, and intellectually ahead or they may be advanced in their motor skills. All aspects are equal (DES 2007; City of Edinburgh Council 2008). Intelligence is much more than being good at maths or language although of course these competences are important too.

- However, many researchers put IQ scores to a different use. They now retain them as measures of progress to validate or negate their interventions, for example Headstart programmes that aim to compensate children from less privileged backgrounds by providing extra resources and teaching input. IQ scores were one way to find if early gains were sustained over time. This is different from using early scores to allocate children to different teaching groups or to make other prognoses of future achievement.

- A new intelligence test for underperforming but gifted children is being planned for secondary pupils. Items will include discerning relationships and patterns within numbers and non-verbal reasoning tests, i.e. 'items that are not dependent on other influences and knowledge of other subjects' (Prof David Jesson, York University quoted in Lightfoot 2005).

- Checklists of characteristics frequently shown by young pupils can provide detailed insights (for lists see Appendix 2). Recordings can be gathered, dated and reviewed in each setting over a few weeks to see if early prognoses are confirmed. To foster reliability, two or more pairs of eyes should confirm the assessment. Such informal assessments can provide 'evidence' that is less likely to be deemed subjective if the assessment is made by more than one person and if a recognised checklist has been used. A video camera is a newer resource that can be provide a visual record of progress.

- Genetic and environmental factors combine to give each of us a different endowment of each aspect of intelligence. Gardner's (1983) work on identifying eight kinds of intelligence (personal, affective, physical, mathematical, musical, emotional, social and literary) caused practitioners to look beyond the maths and literacy competences usually given priority, to cover a wider range of abilities. Largely as a result of this work, the original question 'how intelligent is the child?' was amended to become 'in what ways is the child intelligent?'. This much more comprehensive question encouraged assessment in every sphere and embraced children with different single or multiple talents. The definition of intelligence itself changed to become 'intelligence is the ability to respond appropriately in different situations'. Can any child do that without being intelligent?

In 2006, Gardner further shared his thinking, claiming that there are 'five kinds of mind'. These are :

1 The disciplined mind, for it is important that children can focus and achieve real mastery in one or more disciplines. This would ensure a sound knowledge base and provide evidence of the commitment and application necessary for high achievement.
2 A mind that can synthesise, that is sift information and select what is pertinent from the mass of information that can confuse the most relevant issues. That information is then pulled together to solve other problems.
3 A mind that is creative so that children can think beyond the ordinary and mundane and devise novel solutions to problem-solving tasks.
4 A mind that is respectful, which lets children value diversity and differences. In response to this, in Scotland the 'R's of education have been renamed as 'respect, relationships and responsive care'.
5 A mind that is ethical, for this allows children to appreciate and act towards the nurturance of others, even at some cost to themselves. This would depend on the development of altruism and empathy or in psychological terms 'a theory of mind'.

Gardner advises Ofsted to avoid testing as 'this is a model that belongs to the past'. The new curriculum, he claims, should be based on developing ethical and respectful minds capable of resonding to issues of global concern e.g. climate change, thus supporting children in the Third World.

When practitioners consider Gardner's criteria, they recognise that if these are the qualities to be observed, then their planning has to provide opportunities for these competences to be demonstrated. If higher-order thinking such as problem solving is to be assessed, then opportunities for the children to be engaged in activities that offer this challenge have to be in every aspect of the curriculum. In organising large apparatus outside or in the gym, as just one example, are there ways of turning ladders and mats so that they do not only suggest straightforward climbing and jumping off? While that is a valuable technical activity that promotes confidence, strength and at least three important basic motor skills (climbing, jumping and landing with control), it does not encourage problem solving. These activities have to engender questions such as: How will I cross from one stage to another? Where will I place my hands/feet to help me to balance? Can I plan a safe route back to the ground? Can I rearrange the apparatus to provide and easier or more challenging path? This is a conceptually different kind of activity, calling on different thinking processes. A good plan will have opportunities for both. And of course such problem-solving experiences can be extended when children work in pairs or groups. Then the question of helping a partner arises and possibly the opportunity to alter the original plan to allow a less able friend to participate. This sounds obvious perhaps, but it is the kind of analysis that would allow practitioners to claim that they were giving experiences to develop respectful and ethical minds (Gardner's fifth and sixth categories).

Similarly to become capable of creative work, tasks need to be sensitively introduced, recognising that children need time, patience, commitment and often a guiding hand to support their work. It is difficult for children to become creative at 2:00–2.30 pm, especially if this is seen as a filler activity. They need time to consider alternative solutions, to build something, even to get it wrong without being blamed. It is a time to enjoy something of one's own and to believe that the learning process will, in time develop into something worthwhile.

Asked to give a list of competences that would fulfil the label 'gifted and talented' Marland (1972) nominates:

- general intellectual ability
- specific educational aptitude

- creative or productive thinking
- leadership ability
- visual and performance arts and
- psychomotor ability (athletics, gymnastics).

While this broader framework is to be welcomed, it does raise questions too. Surely judging 'leadership ability', even when assessed by a professional, is subjective and as such is open to criticism? Is it charisma? Is it bossiness – for children will often cluster around the dominant child? Is it being the biggest or the prettiest – for these attributes are valued highly by four-year-olds? (Bee 2004) Or does the situation define the leader? If a child shows leadership qualities in the playground but much less so indoors, is he still a leader? Practitioners are often beset by such complexities. This is why giftedness and talent are so hard to describe! Marland goes on to claim that these children require differentiated educational programmes beyond what is regularly provided in school (see Chapter 4).

First assessments: children's drawings, what can they reveal?

Most children enjoy drawing and have had some experience of making marks on paper even before coming into the foundation stage/nursery setting. Some years ago the Goodenough 'draw a man' test provided a guide as to how children at school perceived their world and what stage of representation they could produce. Teachers gave children one point for every detail they added to the figure. This was a culture-free assessment as presumably all children had seen a variety of people in their lives. It is interesting to note also that all children seem to pass through the same stages of conventional representation for example drawing a person begins with stick arms and legs coming out of a large head or a house as a square box with a central door, four windows and a chimney with smoke. This is strange given that most children's homes are no longer like that, but it meant that assessments could be quickly made.

The initial test stimulated in-depth studies of children's drawings. Teachers analysed the skills needed to reproduce a recognisable drawing and recorded the age they were achieved. Therapists on the other hand sought to diagnose children's emotional states so what began as a quick check in many settings, became an analytic study. Let's look at just three (Figures 0.1–0.3).

Figure 0.1 Catriona, aged 4 years 7 months

Figure 0.2 Catriona, aged 6 years 1 month

Figure 0.3 Jasmine, aged 4 years 8 months

Glancing at the first drawing, it might not seem particularly impressive but the caption written by a pre-school four-year-old, 'men love women' then it becomes obvious that this child has a gift in literacy! Perhaps she was not motivated to draw a picture? This same child newly six also produced the second drawing of a Victorian lady pushing a pram with a baby. Look how the head and shoulders turn and the wheels on the pram are there too (children draw what they know is there!) That topic sustained her attention and she produced a remarkable picture.

The third drawing is another by a four-year-old with an uneven profile of development. The detail and proportions are amazing. Yet that child was having difficulty interacting with her peers at that time. The teacher scribed the child's words, but the drawings show that the child had assimilated the ongoing work on recognising facial expression.

These two children fulfilled the criteria for being gifted and talented and this was reflected in other areas of their work.

Some pointers about development in gifted and talented children

- Children's early opportunities and experiences may affect their ability to 'perform' in school, but usually gifted and talented children overcome early hurdles quickly, especially if their abilities are spotted and nurtured. Some will succeed despite seemingly overwhelming disadvantages, for example Beethoven, and learning differences, for example Bill Gates!
- The rate at which the different intelligences mature is different and especially in the early years, there can be a gender bias e.g. boys may be slightly slower than girls at fine motor skills, particularly writing because the language centre in the brain tends to be myelinated later in boys (see Chapter 2). So early assessments should always consider maturation.

Figure 0.4 Harry's expression suggests he is not ready for this formal writing experience

- There is no limit to intelligence. The brain has a huge capacity to learn, but in many children progress may be by 'stops and starts.' Children need time to develop ideas and have a wealth of experiences before they can make assessments of their work. Practitioners need to be wary of making judgements too soon.
- Any intervention and/or provision of resources in the setting must be carefully planned and be appropriate. Observation to get inside the child's thinking is vital. If practitioners are unsure, it is best to keep back and keep observing!
- Many practitioners are frustrated by being told that their children need trips and visits to extend their experiences. This is especially true in disadvantaged areas, where there is rarely enough money to make this happen.

Vital too are the ways practitioners interact with the children. Often giving them extra time to consider alternatives is helpful. Indeed bright children can be thwarted by having to move on to another activity too soon. It is important not to ask question after question, or even inadvertently suggest what might come next or what might prove to be a better way. This is incredibly difficult but the ownership must stay with the children! Inappropriate interventions, even intervening at all can interrupt the children's thought processes. Polite ones will defer to the practitioners for they know best, is that not true?

Should gifted and talented children in the early years be given a 'label'?

This is a difficult question. Certainly many children with specific learning difficulties advise us to give them a label. In fact they claim it is their right to know exactly what is wrong so that everyone can recognise that difficulties are not their fault (Jackson 2004). But as there is no definite cut-off point to differentiate between those children that have a condition, borderline cases can be hard to call. Parents too often speak of the relief of having a label because they can be assured that 'bad parenting' is not the cause. Armed with a label, they can seek out information about strategies that can reduce the child's difficulties and share these with the teachers in school. So at the other end of the spectrum should the same argument apply?

Asked about giving labels designating children as 'gifted or talented', practitioners in the early years seem doubtful that this is advisable (Macintyre 2008 – ongoing research into practitioners' views on labelling). They point to the many variables that can impinge on a child's development, for example illness, family upset, different people making the assessments, assessing different things, and conclude that having such a label can be stressful if early gifts and talents are not sustained. They point out that development is not a smooth path and that both temperament and maturation can change initial assessments. Yet many gifted children wish their status to be recognised: 'I like being the cleverest – I can read and write and the children in my class can't – it's good to be different' (Leah, IQ 140).

Only by acknowledging that there are gifted and talented children present can moves to enhance their specific abilities be put in place. The emphasis on schools developing programmes to foster gifts and talents and the move in some regions to recognise that at least fifteen to twenty per cent of the children have special attributes that need enhanced input, seems to point to differentiating children by label as well as practice. And the children themselves are often delighted to know they are ahead of their peers! This is one more challenging question in the move to ensure that education provides the most appropriate learning for all of our children together, gifted and talented or not!

Chapter 1

Gifted and talented children
Explaining the difference – parents' views

When practitioners are told they are to have gifted and talented children in their setting, they often ask 'What's the difference between the two … and how will that affect my planning?' Or if practitioners themselves *suspect* that some children have outstanding abilities, they want to know whether the children really meet the criteria to assign them to these groups or whether they are just very good in their particular setting. This chapter examines these important questions.

Let's begin by considering two definitions of giftedness. The first is offered by a group of parents. They explain that gifted children have:

> A precious endowment of outstanding abilities, which allows them to interact with the environment with remarkably high levels of achievement and creativity.

The word 'endowment' suggests that these parents believe that their children are born with, rather than acquire the potential to do very well. They have a quality of innateness which is demonstrated when they perform at a level well above their peer group. Sometimes parents who have high abilities themselves expect their children to be of this calibre and they may well be pleased or disappointed when development shows their anticipations have or have not been met. Other parents can be surprised, even overwhelmed by their child's ability and wonder 'where did that come from?' (see Chapter 2). They soon learn that genetics can throw up lots of surprises!

Interestingly, parents often recognise how their children's abilities interact with what they experience in their lives. They know that their children are 'empowered by acquired characteristics' i.e. that the children who already have the potential also learn readily and positively from their environmental experiences. These might be early and sustained bonding with their parents that leads to stability and security and/or having positive role models at home, in a care setting, in nurseries and schools. This definition would also suggest that such children had access to a range of stimulating learning experiences at the most beneficial or critical learning time. These might involve them in play, in communicating with adults and other children to make decisions or in being encouraged to think of alternative solutions to problems. Or the children might challenge their motor skills playing out of doors, so learning to balance, co-ordinate and control their bodies and any equipment necessary to develop games skills. From these experiences they develop independence and learn to take confidence-building risks. These are much more demanding experiences than just being told what to do.

The 'acquired characteristics' could also mean being motivated enough to continue probing when solutions are difficult to find or being prepared to take part in group competitions. These might just give children who find most things easy, experiences in losing and learning to do so with grace! A variety of opportunities provide opportunities to shine but also times to recognise that other children have gifts that shine in different arenas. So they find that that they are not alone in being a high achiever. Through such activities the children develop a positive but realistic sense of self, which is the basis of self-esteem.

So, is giftedness something parents always welcome? What do parents say?

Listen to Anya talking about her son Calum, Jake speaking of his daughter Marie and grandparents Leah and Brad speaking of their grandchild, Amy. First Anya.

Calum is four now and even at this early age, it's very difficult to give him the stimulation and the education I feel he needs. While I have to be pleased he is so bright, sometimes I wish he was just ordinary. All the time, and no matter what the rest of the family is doing, he asks questions and he's never content with the answers. I know children ask 'why' all the time but Calum's questions are different; they are much more intense. When we are having a meal or trying to watch television his attention is obviously elsewhere. He is so restless. 'Why isn't God married?' he'll ask. 'Does he not have children then? I thought he liked children, doesn't He say so? Is He white or black or brown and why is that? What language does he speak?' and when I say, 'I just don't know' he gets so angry. How do you satisfy such a curious child?

When he was a toddler, I always told him stories, but he was more interested in what each word said rather than the story itself. He'd want to know why some words had more letters than others and he'd challenge words like through and enough wondering how they didn't sound the same. He quickly built up a vocabulary and taught himself to read before he was three. Then he chose what he wanted to read. This was always factual stuff because 'stories are rubbish, just for babies'. So when the other children hear stories at school or even talk about Harry Potter he immediately interrupts with something else. He is very single-minded and determined, even domineering. It's not easy to cross him.

Anya also explained her exhaustion, 'He is always on the go, there's never a minute when we can relax. Thankfully he spends time on the computer looking up sites on the Internet, but that's a worry too because he's learning more and more and how will the teacher cope? How will he make friends if he always knows best? How will I manage when he comes home?'

Anya concerns show that having a gifted child can be a hard act to manage!

Jake's daughter Marie had a different way of coping with her gifts. Jake recalls:

Marie finds learning things very easy, but she has a social maturity that helps her to interact with all the children round about. She goes out to play quite happily; to outsiders she usually appears happy and content. She seems to be popular because the other children come to play and ask her what games they should play, things like that. She always smiles and includes everyone, that's why they keep coming, I think.

The only downside I see to her being so bright is that she gets so worried about children in the Third World. How many other four-year-olds would know about their hardships I wonder? I've explained that when she's older she can visit these countries and help the children. I thought that would allow her to put sad thoughts aside for now but she seems to be investigating even more. It's as if she has two personalities. When she's with children she's carefree and at home she gets worried and morose. She understands these mood swings and says they happen because she thinks too much. What should I do? When she heard a programme on climate change, she asked if we would get poorer as we got hotter. Then she seemed glad because, 'That'll let people feel what it's like in Somalia'.

A thoughtful sense of humour was part of Marie's personality too!

Now Amy. Amy lives with her grandparents. They were enchanted by Amy's gift for music. Her grandmother explained, 'What a wonderful sound her piano makes – she makes the notes sing and she wants to practise all the time. It gives her and us so much pleasure.' Asked if and how they had encouraged Amy's talent, her grandmother explained,

Well we are a musical family. We have always enjoyed concerts and my husband was a very good singer. Although he didn't have the opportunity to make a career out of music, that would have been his first choice. But we play music all day in this house, it's really important to us, so we were especially pleased when Amy showed a real aptitude for playing an instrument. She is fully committed to becoming a concert pianist. We never have to ask her to practise. She would stay at the piano all day if she could. She's looking forward to the proms on television and for a special treat we'll take her to the Albert Hall to hear the orchestra there.

Asked whether they were concerned that Amy's focus on music made her education rather narrow, her Grandfather replied,

> Well, a gift is one thing, but even with a gift, she needs to practise. Even Mozart needed to practise. She has a wonderful teacher who gives her so much encouragement but even when she is not available Amy keeps working. You can't water down a gift for music by insisting she does something she wouldn't enjoy so much – where's the sense in that?

From these case studies it can be seen that any definition of giftedness must be multi-faceted.

Gagné's definition of giftedness is endorsed by the City of Edinburgh Council (2001) in its document *A Framework for Gifted and Talented Pupils.* It claims that giftedness is,

> The possession of untrained and spontaneously expressed natural ability in at least one ability domain – that would place the child in the top 15 per cent of the age group.

Again it involves the notion of giftedness being 'spontaneously expressed' as if no training or education was needed to make the child shine. And it emphasises that children can be gifted 'in just one ability domain, or aspect of their development'(rather than having to be high achievers all across the board, i.e. intellectually, socially, emotionally and in the motor domain). Colloquially this is known as 'garden-variety gifted'. This highlights the importance of practitioners observing and assessing i.e. giving equal attention to all aspects of the children's development (see Appendix 3) but while all aspects interact, separating them out makes observation and assessment easier.

While the English model offers the description that 'gifted and talented children are those who have one or more abilities developed to a level significantly ahead of their year group – or the potential to develop these abilities' (DCSF 2005), and aims to give all children 'work that challenges stretches and excites them', they allow the schools to 'define their own population'. In so doing the model asserts that a 'school's gifted and talented cohort should be broadly representative of the school's population'.

Table 1.1 Characteristics of gifted children identified by families compared to expert lists. Note that all gifted children would not be expected to register on all of the items, rather on a high proportion of them.

Families	Expert lists
Asks unusual questions	Learns easily
Perseveres – debates answers	Original, imaginative, creative
Demands attention	Persistent, resourceful, self-directed
Interrupts frequently	Inquisitive, sceptical
Wide vocabulary	Informed in unusual areas
Self-taught reading	Artistic: Good physical control
Single minded / Determined	Outstanding vocabulary: verbally fluent
Very active – always on the go	Musical
Socially mature – can relate to adults well	Independent worker: takes the initiative
Leadership qualities	Good judgement: Logical
Empathises with others	Shows unusual insights
Thinks too much	High levels of sensitivity and empathy
Committed to practise	Excellent sense of humour

Source of expert list: Dept of Education and Science (1992)

A difference is that in the English model the term 'gifted' refers to pupils who are capable of excelling in academic subjects such as English or history. 'Talented' refers to pupils who 'may excel in areas requiring visual-spatial skills or practical abilities such as those required in PE, drama or art'.

Current priorities state that there should be a trained 'leading teacher for gifted and talented pupils' for each cluster of primary schools and that tracking the progress of such pupils will be an important development.

So does a gifted child need anything beyond ability? And are there downsides to being gifted? Gagné points out that 'Motivation and a healthy self-esteem are essential if giftedness is to become talent' (City of Edinburgh Council 2001).

This proviso alerts parents and practitioners to the effect of the children's motivation on their capacity to fulfil their potential. While the children described above were certainly motivated, even to the point of obsession, some gifted children seem to be content not to use their gifts, especially if they prefer to do other things or perhaps nothing at all!

It can be very hard to stimulate intrinsic motivation if the children do not value the set tasks and if they have worked out that what they are being asked to do is of little relevance to their own goals.

Silverman (1993) describes other personality characteristics that might work against the demonstration of intrinsic gifts. These are 'intensity, questioning rules/non-conformity, a preference for isolation and perfectionism' and they highlight the fact that gifted children may have problems accepting usual ways because they can think at a level beyond the commonplace. So they may work out the lack of logic behind some rules and resent having to conform. They may also be so intrigued by their own project that they find it unreasonable to share their ideas and inventions or finish what they are doing before they are ready just because the routine of the day requires that they do so. This attitude, frustration, even aggression, does not help them make friends. So practitioners have to recognise that these children may become socially isolated and there may be conflict with the school staff as well as with the pupils themselves.

These difficulties can also impact negatively on children's self-esteem which fluctuates, particularly when the children are very young. It is continuously being formed by the impressions the children have of how they are regarded by the important people, the 'significant others' around them. So if they realise that teachers and pupils find them 'different' in any way, the children may take steps to fit in with the crowd and resent overtures that single them out such as giving them differentiated work, asking them for too many answers or asking them to oversee the work of less able pupils (Naisbitt 2001).

Does developing a high self-esteem depend on what the gift is?

Ongoing investigations into how parents talk about their children's gifts and talents are discovering that parents of gifted children were more likely to share that news with others if their children's gifts were of the musical or sporting variety (Macintyre 2008). They were less likely to comment to other parents that their children were very good at maths or literacy, as a result children who were gifted and talented in these areas didn't hear the comments being shared and so didn't realise that their parents were proud of their intellectual gifts. And so they were less convinced that their abilities were good to have! Interestingly in popularity studies, children who were good at sports were the ones nominated at the top! Is there a cultural modesty that is causing parents and children to have priorities?

This second part Gagné's quotation (City of Edinburgh Council 2001) also raises the issue of defining talent. So what is 'being talented' and how does this differ from being gifted?

> Talent is achievement in any field of performance that puts the pupil in the top 15 per cent – one who performs at a significantly higher level than might be expected...

Again the top 15 per cent of children are identified. But while giftedness is seen as potential, which may or may not be realised, talent is achievement. It depends on children working hard. There must be a certain level of ability but the level of success depends on the level of commitment.

However, there are some eminent educationalists (such as Donald McIntyre, until recently Professor of Education at Cambridge University) who advise that any child can do anything provided they are committed enough! While this gives pause for thought, Winner (2007) disagrees. She explains that the level of commitment required 'is just not possible if the child does not have a high level of ability'. She speaks of a four-year-old who loves to practise the piano for six hours every day and she is sure that 'you just can't make an "ordinary" child fulfil this demand'.

Another difference between giftedness and talent is in the 'untaught' element. Talent comes in response to dedicated practice and because there is a technique involved – i.e. learning how to do something complex – it depends on skilled training. Usually an experienced tutor or coach is required before the talent emerges to the level that gives outstanding success.

So children can be gifted and talented, gifted without being talented and/or talented without being gifted!

Gagné's model of giftedness and talent

Gagné differentiates between giftedness and talent in diagrammatic form (see Figure 1.1). He sees giftedness as 'aptitude' and identifies four key domains

The intellectual domain

The first domain is 'intellectual' and Gagné suggests that giftedness in this domain is seen in the children's powers of logical reasoning. Children gifted in this domain readily understand that there may be more than one point of view and can visualise alternatives. They understand that different people may have different perspectives. So the children are able to sift from a mass of incoming information and quickly weigh up appropriate and alternative ways of responding. This capacity would lead to an efficient and effective means of solving problems.

These children must also be able to transfer what they have learned to other situations so that knowledge is not only something to be gained for its own sake, rather it leads to understandings that have wider applications. Children with Asperger's syndrome may well build up knowledge but not have the ability to transfer that to other situations.

Gagné is defining the underlying abilities that enable the child to solve problems across different fields through using the frontal cortex or executive centre of the brain (see Chapter 2). This is quite different from being good at school subjects – for example, literacy or maths – it's more an application of a way of thinking, rather than meeting school targets, although of course these skills are important too and may have been the first things to alert parents and teachers to a child's high potential.

Good memories

To learn easily depends on having a good memory. Meadows (2002) explains that 'remembering of some sort is necessary for virtually all human cognition'. If children can remember, they can build new learning on what has gone before with out too much recap or time spent on overlearning/repetition. And, as having a poor short-term memory is part of every special need or additional support condition, is it realistic to claim that a good memory is essential to being gifted?

There are different kinds of memory that have specific jobs to do (see Figure 1.2). In developmental terms, the improvements in memory from infancy to adulthood have been coined as:

1 an improvement in basic capacities such as memory size;
2 development in the use of strategies e.g. grouping, repetition, to aid remembering;
3 changes in children's own understanding about how their memories work (metamemory), allowing them to use the most relevant associations; and
4 more knowledge of the environment that allows them to make connections or build sensory pictures to make the event memorable.

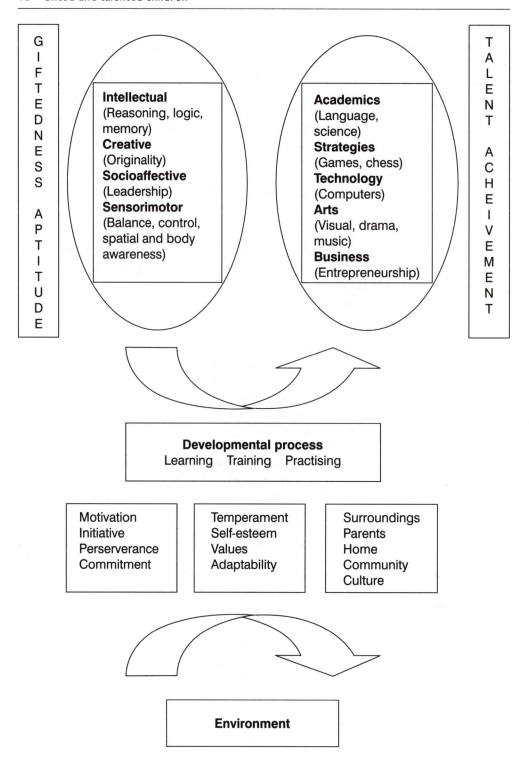

Figure 1.1 Gagné's model of giftedness and talent (source: City of Edinburgh Council 2001)

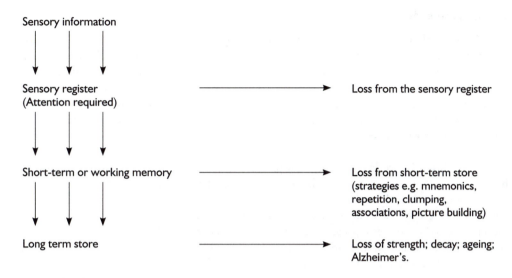

Figure 1.2 The process of remembering

How does the memory work?

Information comes from the senses into the sensory register and stays there for a short time. Some is discarded, but some passes into the short-term memory store and then to the long-term memory. Both the sensory register and the short-term store are limited in size, so strategies have to be used if events are to pass to the long-term memory (see Figure 1.2). Understanding this has implications for teaching, for the rate and pace of giving new material, and for explaining and embedding the use of repetition into lesson plans.

Each memory store uses control processes on the information it contains. In the short-term store, rehearsal or repeating items over and over again, e.g. rote learning rhymes, stops items being lost and helps transfer them into the next stage. The short-term store takes information from current and retained experiences and by building new strategies, for example by making associations or building visual pictures, helps pass the important information to the long-term store.

As children grow older their memory space increases. So they become more able to operate more processes at once and so their cognition improves. It is important that teachers appreciate the processes and strategies involved in remembering so that they can nurture good memories and help children to use alternative strategies if one aspect of their memory lets them down.

Interestingly, savants, who along with a learning disability have prodigious memories for numbers, timetables or calendars, deny that they go through these processes to memorise vast stores of information. In the television series 'The Brilliant Brain' (2007) Professor Alan Sneider claims that the disability has 'knocked out' the left side area of the brain leaving the right side dominant. So the part that identifies detail takes over to aid memorising. He experimented by using magnets against a student's left brain to impair its functioning and found that responses to tests before and after the intervention were markedly different. The post-intervention results included an increase in the ability to draw in detail and stimulated focus so that the student read passages slowly and accurately, rather than skimming words in the usual manner. In giftedness in the creative domain, he explains, 'the right side of the brain, known as the artistic creative side, must withstand the normal and possibly inhibiting strength of the left'. A fascinating experiment indeed, only made possible by the knowledge that the effects of the magnet wore off after a short time leaving the student with both sides of his brain functioning as before!

The creative domain

Gagné's second domain is the 'creative' one and to fulfil this criterion of giftedness children must be able to conjure up novel ways of completing a task. They must be innovative in their approach, working with materials or ideas to produce something that is different. But of course just anything that is different will not do. The result must be appropriate in the context of what was required. But even if what children are producing does not meet their expectations, practitioners can listen to them explain their intentions and anticipated outcome. But of course the children must have the opportunity to experiment and self-assess as well as the time and resources that make innovative work possible (see Chapter 4).

There is always danger that a well-meaning practitioner can spoil children's original work, possibly by imposing their own ideas or standards. Somehow they feel conditioned to approach children and ask questions such as 'what's that?' when to the child either 'what it is' is patently obvious, or the artefact hasn't reached the form where it needs a name. In either case the child, in trying to please the adult, often loses ownership and interest in what was being made. In a fantasy world, especially, children need time and patience to bring their creativity to life. Unless adults are sure that their thinking is in line with the children's thought processes, it is better not to intervene.

There is some debate about using the term 'creative' to describe young children's work. Some would argue that the term 'imaginative' would be more appropriate. This is because children's lack of experience and technical know-how usually limits their efforts. Such purists uphold the idea that creative works must be able to stand extended scrutiny by an expert in the particular field and they debate whether any young child could produce work of this calibre. But either term requires a novel response that is appropriate in the given situation, not just any one that happens to be different. Most of the children deemed creative are right-brain dominant (see Chapter 2).

Torrance (1972) differentiated between convergent and divergent thinkers. Convergers respond best to questions that require one answer and they tend to stay with the information that is given. This kind of ability suits quizzes, items in many intelligence tests or multiple-choice answers in exams – situations where one rapid-fire answer is required. The divergent thinkers' strength, however, comes in offering various solutions to set problems. To do this they will have had to consider many possible scenarios. This takes time and a broader consideration of possibilities.

Children who are divergers are more creative and tests have been devised, for example, the uses of objects test, to find how these children score. So, items such as 'how many ways could you use a brick, or a cardboard box or a paper clip' have been used in tests. Another example is to give children a page of circles and to ask them to develop them in any way they like. Some fill in each circle separately and others combine the circles to make spectacles or bicycles or barrels. But is one more creative than the other? Therein comes the rub. It is difficult to score any such test and generally there is a lack of agreement about what constitutes an original response. So test items may not be judged either reliable or valid.

Experiences like this, however, develop opportunities endorsed in the EYFS document, such as:

- investigating objects and resources by using all their senses as appropriate;
- building and constructing a wide range of objects selecting appropriate resources and adapting their work where necessary and if they are involved in creative group work;
- interacting with others, negotiating plans and taking turns in conversations (see ideas for dance, art and music in Chapter 4).

The socioaffective domain

This involves understanding the feelings of others in a social context and acting to nurture them.

Being socially aware and being able to appreciate how others are feeling is at the root of being able to treat others with respect. This, in turn, is the essence of building relationships and giving and receiving responsive care.

While everyone wants every child to be happy at school, some children make friends easily and some, often for no apparent reason, get left out. It is fascinating to try to understand what makes some children natural leaders. Some are clever or sporty or musical or artistic, but some have an aura or charisma that doesn't seem to depend on any particular ability. In their research into 'popular children' and the type of leadership envisaged as being acceptable to other children, Parkhurst and Asher (2002) offer the list of characteristics shown in Table 1.2. Some of the things that make early years' children likely to be chosen by others are out with their control. In particular, larger and physically attractive children are sought as friends. But soon, towards middle childhood, it is the way the child behaves that influences popularity.

But when do children develop empathy and altruism, i.e. looking out for others, even at some cost to themselves? Is this something that develops over time or is there a gene that makes some people more caring than others?

Children who are kind to others, for example, giving over a toy that they particularly want to play with or sharing genuine feelings of sadness when a friend's pet dies, are demonstrating prosocial behaviour, the kind of behaviour that wins friends. This competence develops over time like other aspects of development and may depend on the role models the children have had or the guidance they have heard. Practitioners can be frustrated when parents advise their children, 'if he hits you, hit him back harder and he'll not do it again'. These children are having conflicting messages about how to cope with aggression from others and this is hard for them to understand, especially if the gentler advice given by the setting doesn't immediately work!

Interestingly, those children who have developed altruism and empathy are more likely to be those who are able to regulate their own emotions well. And this is not always the case with gifted children who may have a higher level of frustration to match their higher level of intelligence. Normally, altruistic behaviours are first seen at age 2 or 3, i.e. at the time when children begin to play with other children, and of course gifted children may be less likely to find these encounters satisfying. At that age children understand enough about the emotions of others to comfort them when they are sad and this 'comforting zone' is most prevalent in nursery-age children. But children in this very young age group generally are less generous than the older ones. Eisenberg (1992) explains, 'If you describe a child as needy, school-age children will donate more than their younger friends'. This shows that children's understanding of the plight of others (the development of a theory of mind) is a developmental process. So perhaps children gifted in this domain will be popular because they are ahead of the others in detecting their anxieties and responding to their needs?

Children on the autistic spectrum are not usually able to appreciate the feelings of others and this lack often results in them being isolated because the other children don't understand what appears to be an uncaring attitude. One little boy with autism who saw his sister tumble in the playground rushed over to his mother and asked, 'What face will I put on?' He knew that a certain response was required but had no idea what it was or how to make it happen.

Socioaffective learning particularly develops the EYFS competences:

- gaining security through being special to someone: being affirmed by someone special in their lives;
- being able to form caring attachments with children in the group.

Table 1.2 Characteristics of popular children. Some of the things that make early years' children likely to be chosen by others are out of their control. In particular, larger and physically attractive children are sought as friends. But soon, towards middle childhood, it is the way the child behaves that influences popularity.

Popular children	Rejected children
Behave in supportive ways	Taunt and tease others
Explain things	Dominate with their ideas
Accept the wishes of others	Are aggressive if they are thwarted
Are modest; refrain from boasting	Are uncooperative and disruptive

Source: Parkhurst and Asher (2002).

And to achieve this, practitioners are advised to act as role models who value differences and who take account of different needs and expectations.

The sensorimotor domain

Children gifted in this domain are the ones who have developed the key competences of balance, co-ordination and control. They reach their motor milestones early (30 per cent earlier than other children – see Appendix 2) and generally they are strongly built with the muscle power to try out movement challenges. They derive great enjoyment from their success and because their achievements are public, they gain the admiration that perhaps children gifted in maths or language miss. This spurs them to further effort. They have a repertoire of basic movement patterns early on and this allows them to expand their horizons, venture into places and solve problems (for example, how do I get up stairs, or how do I empty cupboards), that others come to later. They can also habituate (that is, transfer their learning from one situation to another), thus enlarging their bank of skills.

A key indicator of ability in the sensorimotor domain is that of being able to use feedback from one try to improve the next. Children who are not skilled will often repeat the same mistakes in their movements and become discouraged. The able ones, however, are able to analyse what went wrong and adjust their next attempt to jump higher or run faster or kick the ball more accurately. Most children gifted in this area have the body build and musculature that supports success and because activity releases endomorphins into the bloodstream, they have the feel-good factor that encourages them to continue trying (see Chapter 2). They are also physically fit children perhaps because of the restlessness that keeps them on the move. Furthermore, being able movers often involves the children in taking risks. In the early years these risks are usually supervised, but the achievement children feel from being able to cope helps them gain independence. Many practitioners report that confidence gained through movement activities transfers into children being more willing to tackle new learning experiences in class. And, of course, if children are given climbing frames and other challenging equipment they can build circuits and solve problems, i.e. they can be be creative in movement terms too.

Winkley (2004) has demonstrated that the development of fine motor skills also has a knock-on effect. He claims that when children use their fingers to count or to thread beads or to play a musical instrument, this energises the frontal cortex of the brain (see Chapter 2) and firms up useful pathways to facilitate learning.

The EYFS competences developed by engaging children in movement activities (for examples see Chapter 4) are that the children should learn to:

- move with confidence, imagination and in safety;
- move with control and coordination (and above all balance – my addition);
- recognise the changes that happen to their bodies when they are active (see Chapter 2);
- handle tools with control.

These domains are those that Gagné identified as being fundamental to giftedness (see Figure 1.1). He saw the school subjects as coming under the heading 'achievement' and put them into the category marked 'talent'. The developmental process in nurturing talent, he claimed depended on learning, training and practising and on the social environment in which the children were raised (see Chapter 3).

At a theoretical level (for practical suggestions of content, see chapter 4), what are the possible ways of providing gifted children with the kind of input that will challenge them appropriately? At every age and stage there must be a range of stimulating activities, promoting activity and interaction between children and staff. The organisation and time schedule must be flexible so that tasks can be given the amount of time they require and the resources must be readily available to hold the children's interest and suggest appropriate ways of developing their project. And of course feedback from staff must be available when required.

The methods generally suggested to offer gifted children challenge are:

- acceleration;
- enrichment or extension; and
- differentiation.

Acceleration

Acceleration involves moving children to a class above the one suggested by their chronological age. This is the most debated method. But particularly in the early years, although this more cognitively demanding setting may suit the academic abilities, the children may well lack the social confidence and prowess to cope. Sometimes children are moved to an older class for certain subjects, usually maths and/or language, but they are not a real part of that class and, when they come back to their own class, they do not have common experiences to chat about. They can land up isolated in each place, not really belonging to either. Unfortunately this state of affairs can spill over into the playground. Parents of other children can be perturbed as to why their children aren't given this opportunity and resentment can flourish, causing anguish. So acceleration needs to be considered carefully in light of the children's overall development.

Enrichment or extension

Enrichment happens when the normal curriculum is enlarged to take in extra experiences such as visits to local areas of interest, more debates and discussions, perhaps having visitors from different cultural backgrounds, and allowing more time for questions and illustrations than is usually the case. These can offer stimulation to every child. Also without changing the setting, gifted children can have extra tasks and time to research their own interests, perhaps on the Internet. Or they can make displays or support other children. Of course these activities should be available for all the children, but they may be particularly useful for the gifted ones. Sometimes specialists can come into class for extra tuition. Very often careful organisation, rather than extracting the gifted child from the room, can mean that all the children benefit.

Differentiation

This is perhaps the most realistic solution given the pressures on practitioners to cope with twenty or thirty children at once. Differentiation means setting tasks at different levels of challenge. This can be subtly done so that other children do not realise that their work is different. Gifted children may also need more or less time to complete a task and allowing this is another form of differentiation. When other children bring photos from home, perhaps in making a 'this is me' book, the gifted ones can not only use the digital camera but also alter the pictures to give the best display. They might also take pictures to illustrate a theme and their work can be admired, used or discussed by the other children. This does involve practitioners in extra preparation, but once the children know what is possible, gifted ones can often suggest ways in which they would like to progress. Giving them time to explain and really listening to them can make sure that progressions are appropriate and well received by children and their parents.

Chapter 2

Understanding the nature of gifted and talented children

A biological perspective

Is there a gene for genius? Are children born with something extra that their upbringing can't explain?

Over the years there have been many claims about the relative importance of the contributions nature (what children inherit) and nurture (how they are supported in their environment) make to their development. Those who favour the first stance argue that gifted children inherit 'a propensity to do very well', and they ask if there is a gene for genius! The environmentalists, however, ask how these researchers have obtained data to justify such a claim, given that the pre-natal environment is affecting the baby even before it is born.

Professionals in education need to understand the importance of both nature and nurture. First, they need to appreciate how the brain works to enable children to learn. This knowledge helps them recognise what is happening when some children learn with ease and others have mild or profound impediments to their progress. Then they need to appreciate how the inherited competences respond to the many variables in the environment. These interactions make each child unique (DfES 2007).

Heredity and the pre-birth environment – interacting from the start

Bee (2004) calls heredity 'a genetic blueprint that influences what we can do' suggesting that children inherit a pattern of abilities and disabilities that will, to some extent, affect how they learn and behave and make their way in the world. But how does this come about? What are the things we are born with i.e. the things that make up our genetic code? To understand this we need to go right back to the moment of conception when the sperm, the father's contribution, and the smallest cell in the body, travels along the fallopian tube and pierces the shell of the egg, the largest cell, to form the zygote. While all other cells in the body have 46 chromosomes, the ovum and the sperm have only 23 each because these come together to make up the 46 in the zygote. Chromosomes are long strings of molecules in a twisted helix that can be subdivided into genes and these genes are placed at the same place on each chromosome. This allows researchers and clinicians to talk about G6 or G10 and identify the characteristics each gene carries – a fact that helps genetic screening. Geneticists are aiming to modify the effects of genes that carry life-threatening illnesses such as Huntington's chorea and genetic disabilities such as cystic fibrosis.

Sometime during the first 24–36 hours after conception the chromosomes replicate and cell division begins. Tendrils are formed and these implant cells into the uterine wall. This is the start of the embryonic stage. The zygote divides very rapidly and 14 days after conception, the cells that form the central nervous system (CNS) can be found as a ridge on the embryo. This forms into a long tube and the top bends over to form the brain and head.

The combination of genes from the father and from the mother provide a unique genetic pattern and from that moment in time and provided there are no accidents during the time of cell division, (for example, the extra third copy of chromosome 21 causing Down's syndrome) or if there are no negative effects coming from the placenta through the umbilical cord (for example, the mother's supply of oxygen to the baby's red blood cells may be contaminated by smoking or drug abuse; the removal of waste may not be efficient; or illnesses caught during the first three months of pregnancy –

rubella, for instance, may damage the baby's sight and hearing), then the 'nature' side of development is set. Already certain characteristics are there – eye colour, body build, some aspects of intelligence and temperamental traits, for example, whether the child will be outgoing or shy (see also Chapter 3). The genetic blueprint means that from conception the child will have the means to develop certain abilities and/or a likelihood of inheriting learning differences such as dyslexia, dyspraxia, autism, or even more debilitating illness such as haemophilia. So, from conception there are different potentials that affect how readily learning and the emergence of gifts and talents can occur.

As the placenta and other support structures are formed, the embryo is differentiating itself into specialist groups of cells for hair and skin, sensory receptors, muscles, nerve cells and circulatory systems. By the eighth week the embryo is 1½ inches long and already has a heart and a basic circulatory system, and by 12 weeks the child's sex can be determined; eyelids and lips are there and feet have toes and hands have fingers. And for the rest of the period of gestation, the development of the systems goes on.

The nervous system is one of the least well-developed systems at this time; even at birth the baby is relatively helpless compared to other primates. But maturation is clearly at work promoting development. At birth the foetus 'has already been listening for twelve weeks' (Winner 2007) and the baby's kicks are early spatial reckonings that help learning about distance, directions and body boundary, i.e. where the body ends and the outside world begins. This helps orientation and efficient movement after the child is born.

All babies sit before they stand and walk before they run. They don't need to be taught to do these things; there is an inbuilt pattern of maturational changes that are the same for all children in every culture (Trevarthen, 1977). Understanding this sequence of changes allows researchers to collect normative data and so formulate the milestones that guide assessment in the early years. Children who are gifted achieve at least some of these milestones 30 per cent quicker than their peers (see Appendix 2). It is also true that their first environment has not had to deal with toxins or illnesses that might have damaged the developing brain.

Practitioners often wonder how siblings can be so different. This is because each child, even from the same parents, inherits different chromosomal material through the passage of dominant and recessive genes.

Dorminant and recessive genes

When a trait is governed by a single gene inheritance paterns follow rules and the child expresses both characteristics. Many physical characteristics are like this. For example, a child with an AB blood group has inherited type A gene from one parent and type B gene from the other.

More usually one of the two genes is dorminant over the other and only this is expressed. The other, the recessive gene, has no impact on the child's appearance or behaviour but it stays in the genotype.

In the next generation, if a child inherits a recessive gene from both parents, that characteristic is likely to emerge. Characteristics that follow the pattern of dominant and recessive genes are normally 'either/or' … the child has curly hair or not. But many characteristics result from multiple genes, i.e. polygenetic inheritance. Complex traits such as intelligence or personality are examples. Then the influence of the genes has to be inferred from other information such as studies of twins.

However, genetic codes are not set in stone. The outcome is affected by the experiences the child meets from conception on. There are many variables, for example, the parents' age, or diet during pregnancy or the efficiency of the placenta, that can affect the developing foetus too.

The structure of the brain

The brain is much more sophisticated than the most advanced computer because, apart from working at lightning speed, it can appreciate the feelings of others and respond to them in an appropriate way. Some children do this readily, others with difficulty and, sadly, an increasing number of children on the autistic spectrum cannot do it at all. Furthermore the differences in social competence can be

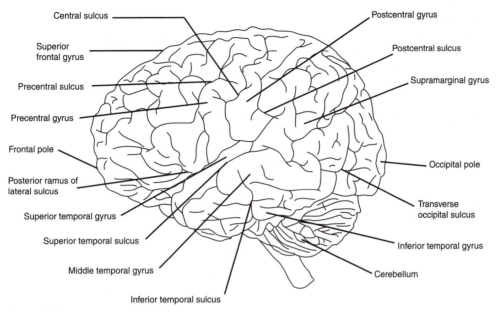

Figure 2.1 The exterior of the brain

echoed in the other aspects of development, i.e. in movement or motor development, in intellectual or cognitive development, and in emotional or affective development. Trying to understand the source of these different levels of ability is a fascinating, complex and even essential study for everyone who wants to really understand how children learn.

Does the structure of the brain impact on a child's ability to learn?

Well, if we were to take out our brains and lay them side-by-side, what would we discover? The first surprising thing would be that they all looked the same. Each would weigh about 1400 grams or 3lbs, i.e. the weight of a bag and a half of sugar. Babies' brains are about three-quarters of the adult size and they grow rapidly until at old age, the tissue shrinks making the brain appear slightly smaller again. About 75–80 per cent of each brain would be made up of water, 10 per cent fat and 8 per cent protein. The brains would appear greyish – white and convoluted and have the unattractive, rubbery consistency of a large mushroom or fungus (see Figure 2.1).

At first glance it might appear that specimens of the most complex structure on the planet all look the same (Winston 2004). There is nothing to indicate that each brain houses different personalities and attributes, different attitudes and temperaments, different gifts, talents and difficulties. There is nothing to show the experiences the children had, whether they were happy or sad, well nourished or deprived, capable or not. So the brains of gifted and/or talented children and those with global developmental delay or specific additional support needs look just the same. In fact Professor Richard Ernst who won the Nobel Prize for his work on magnetic resonance imaging (MRI), had his own brain scanned and was quite miffed to find it was no different to anyone else's! So, given the huge difference in people, the outside structure appears remarkably the same.

Having said that, there are some differences. The grey matter, which is made up of 100 billion neurons or nerve cells, has gyri and sulci (ridges and valleys) and these can differ in size and shape. Interestingly, the surface of the brain appears less convoluted in children with Down's syndrome. Does this lack of complexity explain the intellectual deficit attributed to the condition? Certainly fewer convolutions means that there will be fewer neurons or brain cells making connections via their axons and dendrites to do the thinking and problem solving necessary to cope with life independently at an early age.

Inside the brain there are differences too, and these affect its function. The children's experience can affect the growth of dendrites (see Figure 2.2) and so establ;ish more connections and contracts. Also in boys, the corpus collosum – the tough band of fibrous tissue joining the two hemispheres of the cerebral cortex and facilitating the transmission of 'instructions' from one hemisphere to the other – tends to be smaller. Some researchers claim that this prevents the quick interchange of stimuli between the two hemispheres and as a result boys are more likely to be single-minded than girls who multi-task or do several things at once. This has also been put forward as a possible reason why boys feature much more than girls in the statistics (usually 4/5:1) on additional support needs. But the corpus collosum in gifted children appears larger than normal, so there is more space for messages to pass from one side of the brain to the other and as a result the two sides are able to synchronise the incoming information readily. So the structure impacts on learning in a significant way.

In children with autism, as another example, the amygdala, – the area associated with emotions such as fear and disgust – is shaped differently. Can this explain the differences such as poor imagination and lack of understanding social cues that impact cruelly on those children?

Inside the brain

How does the brain work? The brain is made up of at least 100 billion neurons (nerve cells – see Figure 2.2) all organised into different systems that have particular jobs to do. The cells sense, store and process specific kind of stimuli and as they do they communicate with one another. They take information from the external environment through the senses and from the internal environment (for example, sensations of hunger, joy and pain) then they transmit that to the appropriate area in the cerebral cortex for analysis and follow with a lightning response. In the early stages there are a proliferation of networks, but experience allows useful pathways to be formed and those which are unused to die away and be absorbed by the glial cells. This is known as synaptic pruning of the dendritic arbour.

These neurons (also called nerve or thinking cells) are supported by more numerous glial cells which, as their name suggests, 'glue' or support the network. They also store sugar as an energy source and sustain adequate levels of serotonin – the happy hormone. Glial cells also help in the formation of myelin, a substance that acts as an insulating sheath to ensure the efficient transfer of messages from one cell to the next. It is important to realise that myelin builds up in response to exercise and that it can keep building, initially until children are six years of age and on till adolescence.

As the cells take information from the environment, this is another incidence of early interaction. So children surrounded by music or the sounds of different languages or different movement experiences in a play park are receiving very different stimuli (both number and kind) from those who have little communication with others and who spend much time sitting watching television.

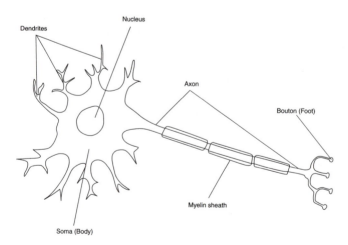

Figure 2.2 A neuron

Critical/sensitive learning times

This maturational process also explains why certain abilities and competences must be stimulated at the right time. Winston (2004) gives the example of a baby born with a cataract. If this is not removed in the first six months, he claims that the baby will never see because the neural pathways have not been primed to react to visual stimuli at the correct time. Unused, they join others with a different function or wither and die. Similarly, achievement in literacy can be impaired when children have had early functional hearing loss. If such children have not heard the difference between sounds at the correct time (for example, between 'p', 'b' and 'd') they may never learn to speak (as is the case of some children with Down's syndrome), or even if they do they will be likely to have spelling and reading difficulties, possibly contributing to dyslexia (Peer 2004). Overlearning and rote learning may have to substitute for intuitive learning, making progress slower and harder for both teacher and child. (See the section on gifted children with learning differences in Chapter 5). This shows the importance of the correct timing and pacing of giving new material. Medical personnel are making progress in making other parts of the brain take over when the usual bases are knocked out by strokes or other illnesses, but this is not ideal for children. The earliest possible detection of sensory difficulties is the answer so that intervention can compensate for any problem.

Sensory input: the first stage in the learning process

> All learning takes place in the brain, but it is the body that acts as the vehicle by which knowledge is acquired. Both brain and body work together through the central nervous system and both are dependent on the senses for all information about the outside world.
>
> (Goddard Blythe 2005)

The continuous chain showing the process of learning is

Sensory stimulus → (CNS) → Analysis and interpretation in the brain → Output or action by the body.

Sensory stimulus

Some difficulties have been explained here to link with the children with asynchronous development in Chapter 5. It is important to remember that gifted and talented children can have sensory difficulties and may use their other abilities to disguise this. So assessment must look beyond the obvious else sensory difficulties will persist.

The sensory system is part of the nervous system. The sensory receptors take information from the external environment through seeing, hearing and feeling (through the visual, auditory and tactile senses and those of taste and smell) and through the internal ones (the vestibular, proprioceptive and kinaesthetic senses). These senses should work together (sensory integration) to facilitate observation, learning and behaviour.

The vestibular sense

The vestibular sense, which controls balance, is at 'the core of functioning' (Goddard 2002) because all other senses pass through the vestibular mechanism at brain-stem level. And so input from all the other senses must be matched to the vestibular before their information can be processed accurately. This is the first sense to function and even in the womb it is working to get the baby in the correct, head down position ready to be born. From then on it functions to control any change in posture or alignment. It helps ascertain hand and foot dominance that is important in writing and in all forms of habitual movement patterning.

The benefits of an efficient vestibular sense are:

- a good sense of balance so efficient movement becomes automatic;

Table 2.1 The senses

The senses	Their key role	Good responses	Indicators of difficulties
Vestibular	Balance	In control in all environments; climbs with ease; can sit and stand still	Unsteadiness; unwilling to leave the ground or take risks
Kinaesthetic	Spatial awareness	Can judge spaces and drops; recognises patterns and shapes	Unable to judge distances; bumping and spilling
Proprioceptive	Body awareness Co-ordination	Well co-ordinated: can crawl using cross lateral co-ordination	General clumsiness; poor muscle tone
Visual	Seeing and tracking (functional sight)	Can follow patterns and track words on the page; not disturbed by flickering lights	Squinting; rubbing eyes; holding a book too near or far from the face
Auditory	Listening and hearing	Can distinguish sounds easily; can cut out distracters; enjoys rhythmical activities	Distractibility; inability to focus; general inattention; covering ears to attempt to block out sound
Tactile	Feeling and touching	Can tolerate touch; welcomes hugs; not annoyed by textures	Needs firm touch or can't bear to be touched; difficulties with personal space
Taste and smell	Accept/reject food	Readily accepts new foods; not upset by smells	Unwilling to try new foods; upset by smells and tastes

- ability to assimilate quick changes of direction;
- enjoyment of funfairs, playgrounds and challenging environments;
- table limbs allow changing position easily;
- ability to stand and sit still – the hardest movements of all.

The vestibular system could be compared to having an internal compass that tells us about directions (forward, up, down, sideways) and allows the body to adapt to changing environments in a controlled manner. This is why observing a child's movement patterns can be an early indicator of high functioning abilities or possible difficulties.

The kinaesthetic and proprioceptive senses

These two names are often used interchangeably, however, to be accurate, the kinaesthetic sense only comes into play when there is muscle contraction, i.e. when the body is moving. The proprioceptive sense, however, works all the time relaying positional information when the body is moving or at rest. The proprioceptors are all over the body in the skin and in the muscles and joints. Receptors are even located in the hair follicles! They literally tell us where we end and the outside world begins, so giving a sense of body boundary and stability. Children who are sure where they are in space derive confidence as well as competence in moving efficiently.

The benefits of a good kinaesthetic and proprioceptive sense are:

- a good sense of poise portrays confidence;
- the child who stands and sits well can breathe properly;
- a good sense of direction;
- safely in control of the body – for example, can stop at the kerb;
- can handle sharp tools safely.

The visual sense

Assessing vision should cover much more than close reading and distance vision that is often the main concern in a simple eye test. Children who 'pass' this can still have difficulties tracking (following the words on a page or the writing on the board). Functional vision depends on maturation of the central nervous system.

Visual–motor integration skills are as important as distance sight. The two eyes have to work together to focus on an image (convergence). Some children with poor convergence will see double images that confuse letter recognition; others will see letters move or overlap on the page and may endure severe eyestrain trying to adjust to the movement. This is Mears–Irlen syndrome and can be helped by coloured overlays or coloured lenses in spectacles. The colours should be chosen by the child working with a specialist in this condition. Some opticians offer this service or they will advise where it can be found. Children also benefit from being allowed to choose the colour of paper that suits them best, because different colours defeat the reflection of light which can dazzle and spoil their work. Some children benefit from reading books that have non-justified print (Barrington Stokes Edinburgh and E Print Blackburn publish books on cream paper and with non-justified print for children in the primary sector).

Children must also be able to adjust their focus so that they can decipher objects and print from different angles and directions. This is called accommodation. The three skills, convergence, accommodation and tracking are all prerequisites for quick identification and reading fluently without strain.

The benefits of a good visual sense are:

*   flowing reading due to ability to track and not losing the place;
*   good letter formation;
*   ability to spot small objects quickly;
*   ability to anticipate changes early.

The auditory sense

During the first three years, the child is listening and learning to tune in to sounds of his mother tongue. After that time it is harder to adjust to the tenor of another language. Obviously, loss of hearing significantly affects learning, but children who 'can hear' may have auditory discrimination problems and these may be the basis of a recognised additional learning need, for example, dyslexia or dyspraxia. If the child cannot hear the difference between 'p' and 'b' or 'sh' and 'th' then both reading and spelling are impaired. Even silent reading is affected because then the child listens to an inner voice – if the sounds are not clear then this process will be affected just the same as in reading aloud.

Hearing too much (i.e. auditory hypersensitivity) can cause as much difficulty as not hearing enough. Children bombarded by sound can have difficulty selecting what they need to hear from the variety of different noises around them. Even in a quiet classroom, some children find hearing the teacher difficult, as they cannot cut out minor rustles and squeaks.

Sounds are transmitted to the language-processing centre in the brain. The right ear is the more efficient. Sounds heard there pass directly to the main language centre in the left hemisphere whereas left-eared children have to pass the sound to the language sub-centre and then through the corpus collosum to the left hemisphere for decoding. This slight delay may put left-eared children at a disadvantage (Goddard 1995).

The benefits of a good auditory sense are:

*   can cope with different levels of sound;
*   hears phonics clearly (helps reading and spelling);
*   sounds in the environment can warn of danger;
*   helps clear articulation.

The tactile sense

Tactility or sensitivity to touch is important in feeding, in communicating and in generally feeling secure. Touch is one of the earliest sources of learning and touch receptors cover the whole body. They are linked to a headband in the brain; the somatosensory cortex, and it can register heat, cold pressure pain and body position. It makes an important contribution to the sense of balance.

Some children have a system that is over-reactive to touch and this causes them to withdraw or be distressed by hugs – responses that most children welcome. This can make them isolated and peers can mistakenly interpret their reactions as snubs. Yet these same children can be 'touchers' seeking out sensory stimulation through contacting others even although they themselves would be distressed by such overtures.

The pain receptors can cause difficulties too. Some children are hyposensitive and may not feel pain or temperature change – they may have a huge tolerance to holding hot plates or going out-of-doors ill-clad in icy winds. And the hypersensitive ones will over-react about injections and visits to the dentist. Some even feel pain when having their nails or hair cut and some cannot tolerate seams in socks. All kinds of problems arise from being hypo- or hyper-touch-sensitive.

The benefits of a good tactile sense are:

- tolerance of being touched;
- pain is recognised and registered appropriately;
- good temperature control;
- enjoyment of contact games and sports.

The senses of smell and touch

The sense of smell is the most evocative of the senses as it can stimulate memories, for example, of a garden visited long ago or a hot summer when the milk turned sour! The sense of smell can also stimulate the hormones controlling appetite, temperature and sexuality. Certain smells can become associated with different situations – the smell of a hospital can conjure up memories of pain; the scent of flowers can recall a happy event such as a wedding or a sad one such as a funeral. The sense of smell is controlled by the thalamus.

The sense of taste depends on the sense of smell, so it is not difficult to understand why children often refuse to accept new foods because they do not like the appearance or the smell. Some of the earliest learning comes through these senses, as during the sensory-motor period the baby will put everything to the mouth. This most sensitive part of the body will tell about the taste and the texture of the object and whether it is hard, soft or malleable as well as whether the taste is pleasant or not!

The benefits of a good sense of smell and taste are:

- children are willing to try new foods;
- they are not upset by the smell of antiseptics or scents;
- they can tolerate floor polishes and other chemical sprays.

Although the senses can be studied separately, they do support each other by working together. A poor sense of smell, as one example, inhibits the ability to discriminate different tastes. This is the basis of sensory integration, for example, hearing the approaching bus lets me judge the speed and allows me to get ready to board even before I see it. However, the balance needed to do so smoothly without stumbling (dynamic balance) can be affected if the visual sense does not complement the vestibular one. This is why sensory integration is often called cross-modal transfer. Reactions may vary according to the type of stimulus, its intensity, its rate and its duration. Most people can only tolerate a shrill sound such as a fire alarm or an intensive light for a short time without distress and sensory deprivation – keeping people in total silence or blackout – has been used as a form of torture leading to insanity.

Sensation and perception: the difference explained

Some children are hyper(over)-sensitive to some or all stimuli while other are hypo(under)-sensitive and this affects their response time, their motivation, their compliance or comfort in different situations. The energy beginning the sensory process is called a stimulus (for example, feeling pain) – but when understanding blends with the stimulus (in recognising that the pain comes from a bad tooth), that is perception. Recognising someone smiling is acknowledging a stimulus; knowing that they are friendly calls for perception – this is a kind of intellectual layering if you like. Some children, such as those with Asperger's syndrome or autism, can acknowledge a stimulus without necessarily perceiving what is meant. Perception can strongly influence behaviour: if a dog is heard growling that is sensation, perception (gleaned from previous experience) allows decision making as to whether to placate the animal or run!

The structure of the brain

The brain is divided into two hemispheres (right and left) joined by the corpus collosum, the band of fibrous tissue already described. Each hemisphere has four important areas with each area or lobe mirrored in the other half. While each lobe has its own key function, the parts are also interlinked and dependent on each other. Although each lobe processes its own chunk of things (Carter 2000), the brain works as an integrated whole rather than as separate components.

At the back of the brain is the occipital lobe largely responsible for visual processing; the temporal lobes around the ears deal with sound processing and language; at the top, the parietal lobes cope with perception of space and partly with movement and touch. The frontal lobes deal with higher-order thinking such as problem solving. They also play a large part in regulating behaviour. As they are the last regions to mature, self-control can increase markedly with age! This might explain why 'the terrible twos' is a stage that passes and why many rebellious teenagers turn into law-abiding, conservative adults!

As the brain develops the different areas mature according to an inbuilt biological timing. At birth the brain stem is fully functional but areas that deal with problem solving, abstract thought and complex language mature later. Myelination begins at three months and continues into young adulthood (Winkley 2004).

The only other structure not replicated in each hemisphere is the pineal gland situated deep inside the brain. Claims are made that its function is to regulate the sleep/waking cycle. It is the body's clock.

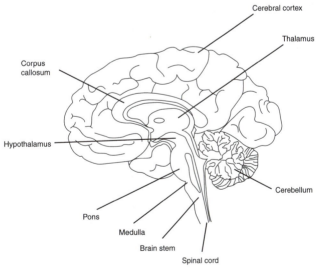

Figure 2.3 A cross-section of the brain

The brain stem

The brain stem is at the top of the spinal column and is part of the central nervous system. It houses the nerve pathways that carry the impulses from the brain to the body. It controls the neurons that regulate the heartbeat, the rate of breathing, body temperature and signals to laugh, swallow or sneeze. Existence really depends on these systems working well. Any severe injury to the core of the brain stem results in death. This is why the first action of a paramedic at the scene of an accident is to stabilise the neck. The brain stem also contains the part where the nerve tracts between brain and body cross over to the other side. The brain stem contains the pons that controls respiration and is associated with arousal and sleep. The pons is a relay centre between the cerebellum and the cortex and the medulla oblongata which controls automatic functions and which is a relay centre between the spinal cord and the brain.

A small number of children with Down's syndrome have cervical instability meaning that cervical vertebrae may dislodge and damage the brain stem. This is why they should not try activities like forward rolls.

Linked to the brain stem is the reticular activating system (RAS), which monitors sensory signals, causing them to stimulate or calm down the sensations in different situations. It is vital in maintaining consciousness and arousal.

The cerebellum

Connected to the brainstem is the cerebellum or little brain, so called because like the cerebral cortex, it has two hemispheres. Although it can't initiate movement on its own, it monitors all the impulses from the motor centres in the brain and from the nerve endings or proprioceptors in the muscles. It coordinates all the input from the senses and so controls every movement. Information from the vestibular sense (balance), from the eyes and from the lower limbs and trunk all pass through the cerebellum. The cerebellum is also responsible for muscle tone, so when it works hard, it helps to strengthen the body (Goddard 2005).

Incoming information from all the senses is vast and the cerebellum sifts out the relevant information and passes it to the correct location for analysis. Some of this information does not get through! There are strong links with the frontal cortex (the part of the brain that deals with problem solving). New research is finding that the cerebellum is more involved with skill development (for example, reading) than was previously thought, but of course reading is a motor skill. Links with memorising are also established. Damage to the cerebellum can cause paralysis in affected regions of the body and dysfunction can cause visual-motor performance difficulties such as dyspraxia and dyslexia. The cerebellum used to be called 'the patron saint of the clumsy child' (Restak 1991).

The part memorising plays can be seen in the dyspraxic child's inability to use feedback from one attempt at a motor task to improve the next. The child without cerebellar dysfunction will reflect and alter the speed, strength or timing of the poor attempt but the children with dyspraxia are likely to repeat the performance that was not successful; the reason being that the cerebellum is not providing the correct cues.

The limbic system

This system is made up of different areas – the amygdala, the hypothalamus, the hippocampus, part of the thalamus and the cingulate gyrus. They are all associated with learning, memory and emotional processing, but currently researchers are disputing their function (Winston 2004). However it has been shown that the number of memory cells is markedly increased in those who are physically active. Activity also releases endomorphins into the bloodstream and also increases the flow of oxygenated blood round the body and the brain. This is why an early activity session each morning helps children concentrate later in the day!

The importance of the memory

To be able to remember is something usually taken for granted and, generally, gifted and talented children are blessed with good memory stores. So they can compare new experiences to those retained in their memory quickly and make judgements and decisions efficiently. They do not need the overlearning recaps of the children with poor short-term memories.

The seat of memory is the hippocampus and if this was not functioning well, everything would appear strange, even homes and friends. This links with the amygdala, which gives meaning to events. Winston (2004) gives the example of seeing a snake. He explains, 'When we see something like a snake, the amygdala contacts the thalamus to produce an instantaneous perception of fear'. If the hippocampus had not stored this memory, then retreat from danger might not be made. So the two work together to keep us safe.

The amygdala

The function of the amygdala is particularly interesting for research into autism. First of all it is shaped differently (Moore 2004) and possibly because of this it biases the children's observations of events. Thus the autistic child urged to recall a motor accident might speak about the red car or the flashing lights, but not be perturbed by or even aware of the personal details such as the pain of the victim or the distress of the onlookers. The amygdala, which responds to four basic emotions, also assigns a label to an object, e.g. 'this is good or bad'. Disorders in the amygdala and its association with the neurotransmitter dopamine may cause the recipient to see more things as bad or threatening and become phobic or depressed.

Dopamine is an important neurotransmitter that helps the smooth passage of stimuli and leads to efficient movement. Its dysfunction plays a major role in a wide range of disorders (Carter 2000). Too much dopamine seems to cause hallucinations, uncontrolled speech and movement (Tourette's Syndrome), agitation and repetitive actions (obsessive compulsive disorder (OCD)). Too little dopamine leads to an inability to initiate movement and tremors (Parkinson's disease and related disorders) and is implicated in depression, lack of attention and withdrawal (Adult Attention Deficit Disorder (AADD)).

The midbrain forms a bridge connecting the lower structures to the cerebrum. It contains the hypothalamus, the basal ganglia and the thalamus, and these centres, with the cerebellum, organise the motor, sensory and autonomic systems. They are important centres for the planning and timing of actions.

The hypothalamus

The hypothalamus, situated just below the thalamus is a synthesiser of the hormones involved in temperature control, water balance, hunger and sexual behaviour. The hormones are fed into the pituitary gland. This gland is often known as 'the leader of the endocrine orchestra' and as such controls the outflow of hormones which affect growth and behaviour. 'Too much hypothalamic stimulation with too little control from the cortex results in the obnoxious child, while the reverse may mean that the child is over-controlled and inhibited' (Goddard 2002). So poor behaviour (as in conditions such as ADHD) may well be out with the child's voluntary control.

The thalamus

The thalamus is an important relay station that carries impulses from the cerebellum and reticular system to the cortex. All the senses (but not the sense of smell) are filtered through the thalamus en route to their specific areas in the cortex. Its main role is in the interpretation of information coming from the senses.

The hemispheres of the cerebral cortex

At the top of the brain is the cerebral cortex, made up of two hemispheres linked by the corpus collosum.

The two hemispheres have complementary specialist skills with a fundamental difference between them in the way they process information. The relationship between the two hemispheres is complex and interacts at many levels in completing a task. They are interdependent through the corpus collosum, and when one side does not function well – perhaps as the result of a stroke – specific training can help the other side to take over. There may, however, be loss of aspects of the function e.g. cadence or variation in tone in speech that has been regained.

Colloquially the two sides have been called 'left for literal, language and listing'; 'right for creative thinking, visualising pictures and seeing holistically' (overviewing the whole picture rather than focusing on the detail), but more and more recognition of the function of the corpus collosum leads to the claim that both sides are involved together to facilitate a response to any instruction.

Nonetheless, brain imaging studies confirm that the two hemispheres really do have quite specific functions (Carter 2000).

The left hemisphere

The left hemisphere is analytical, logical and precise. It processes information as discrete units in linear sequential time. It is dominant for language skills and for fine motor control of the fingers. Language skills cover receptive and expressive speech, reading, writing, spelling, verbal memory and analytic reasoning. This hemisphere copes with voice information. The left side is better at analysing information so it readily identifies details (Winkley 2004).

The right hemisphere

The right hemisphere, which picks up visual cues, is dominant in social functioning, in dealing with emotions and creative, holistic thinking. It overviews the context and so can make judgements about social interactions. It appreciates music and the arts and so it is commonly regarded as the artistic and creative side of the brain.

The right brain is more emotional than the left and is responsible for sad feelings. The creative child (right dominant) is often considered less organised and tidy because the plethora of solutions to a task overwhelm the organisational demands of the left!

Working together

Goddard (2002) explains that if the two parts of the brain were used in isolation, and the person was asked to pick out a previously known person in a crowd, the left side would systematically search, lining up the faces one by one till it picked out the correct one. Then the face would be named. The right side would scan the faces, pick out one, but would be unable to say who it was. The right side is often thought of as the practice ground for skills – they are then passed to the left side to be named. In learning to read there is a time at around seven years when there is a shift to the left side. This is Piaget's stage of conservation and it is now recognised that around this time there is a vast increase in myelination of the axons. Acknowledging this is at the root of moves to delay formal education till children are seven. Children in Norway benefit from this as their results later on show, but still the UK seems unwilling to adopt this model.

Greenfield (2007) claims there is no justification for naming children 'left brainers' or 'right brainers'. She explains:

> Humans have evolved to build a picture of the world through our senses working in unison, exploiting the immense interconnectivity that exists in the brain. It is when the senses are activated together that brain cells fire most strongly and the most efficient learning occurs.

She brushes aside the notion of learning styles claiming that children should develop a flexible repertoire from which they can select the most appropriate response to fit the context. This surely is a sign of intelligence? Many gifted children appear to do this with ease.

So is there a gene for genius? While some children seem to be born with an innate potential to do well and have the motivation and temperament to succeed, the most fortuitous outcome will require the experiences and opportunities to nurture the children and enhance the outcome. Having said that there are those that have overcome seemingly overwhelming disadvantages to bring us music, art, dance, technology and all the things that enrich our existance. Some children have a compulsion to succeed.

Chapter 3

Understanding the nurture of gifted and talented children

An environmental perspective

Can, and in what ways does, the environment contribute to or deter children from being gifted and talented? Do children themselves choose the environment that fosters their specific ability? Can genius be trained or, in other words, can any child achieve anything if they want it enough?

Environmentalists are those that consider the 'nurture' aspect of development to be of major importance. They explain that a balanced approach to explaining giftedness and talent must recognise the environmental and social forces that impact on development before babies are born and throughout their lives. This must have some truth for even committed geneticists do not usually claim that an inherited combination of genes fully determines the outcome. Freeman (1980) widens the environmental impact when she points out 'giftedness varies across cultures and cannot be viewed apart from its social context'. This stance embraces all lifestyles and the different abilities that are valued in varied locations. It could mean between cultures, e.g. the rain forest and built-up urban life or between different social groups in what is seen as the same culture, for example, the 'footballers wives' in Britain and those who have barely enough resources to exist. It is acknowledging these differences in the life skills and abilities that are needed and valued in different cultures that makes the definition of intelligent behaviour, ' the ability to respond appropriately in different situations', absolutely pertinent. This also explains the anomie or unsettled time that most children encounter before adapting to a new environment. In fact 'how quickly they settle' might just be an indicator of intelligence.

The new '3Rs': respect, relationships and responsive care (Scottish Executive 2006)

This wider social definition (particularly used in Scotland, but implicit in all teaching,) supports the philosophy of inclusion, that every child, no matter the social background or the academic ability, should have an education that is based on respect for all cultures, all abilities, learning differences and disabilities. The aim is that this stance will foster positive relationships and will enable all children to achieve through giving and receiving responsive care. Another proviso is that this should happen in the same setting. This philosophy is very different from the old 3Rs, which stressed 'reading, writing and arithmetic'. To fulfil these newer educational aims children must be helped to 'respond appropriately' on both a personal and practical level, in other words, be supported in developing the skills and abilities that will enable them to be successful in their setting and allow them to adapt their responses – transfer their learning – when that situation changes. This premise is also at the root of the different compensatory social/educational programmes offered to try to give all children the same chance to succeed in school, that is, to start them off on a level playing field. Educational researchers aim to find what sort of input is required, when and where it should happen, how long an input can/should last and then, once time has passed, whether initial cognitive benefits from, for example, early literacy programmes, or health benefits from free fruit initiatives or active children programmes, endure once the initiative is over.

Programmes for children with learning differences, different education needs caused by syndromes and other disabilities have also been developed all over the country to try to give these children (who may or may not come from advantaged backgrounds) the education that will allow them to overcome their 'nature' difficulties. At the other end of the spectrum there have been initiatives for gifted and talented children so that they receive more challenging work with peers of similar abilities. More and more, especially if 'inclusion' is paramount, these opportunities have to happen in mainstream settings. But of course this puts extra demands on professionals. They have to understand much more than the content of the programmes they are offering. They have to appreciate the different home and community influences on each child; recognise the peer group pressures and the less savoury aspects such as bullying that can occur, especially when children are seen to be different. They also have to consider how each child's temperament and developing self-esteem impact on how they react to the teaching and the relationships that are part of everyday living.

When do environmental influences begin?

The first environment

It seems strange to talk about social interaction before a child is born, but in nowadays new mothers are being encouraged to talk to their unborn child. This is because mothers report, and scans show, that the foetus responds to the mother's voice by becoming still and listening. Responding like this is a sure sign that the babies are hearing, learning and communicating even before they are born! One mother whose son had a prodigious musical talent had played classical music constantly for him before he was born. Would this gift have developed without this intervention? Or did this promote the genius he was found to have? Or was early exposure to music post-natally the cause? How can one tell? However, if effects like this can be proved, perhaps developing interaction skills as well as healthcare advice will become part of antenatal care for all mothers-to-be?

The baby's kicks also tell the mother and the midwives that the baby is developing well, so that is another social message of reassurance. Interestingly, the kicks usually elicit some 'conversation' from the mother – 'Wow, the footballer is practising again!" – and encourage other family members to 'have a feel'. In this way the baby becomes ' a real person' rather than just a bump. Perhaps this kind of interaction has a real benefit? One mother, Sue, recounts:

> When the health visitor asked, 'Have you felt the baby move?' and I answered, 'I'm nearly black and blue inside!' we laughed out loud, but it was then that I realised that I would soon have a real live baby to look after. At that moment I felt a surge of love for the baby. It sounds weird but it wasn't till that moment that I thought of my baby as a real person. I had had a scan but I couldn't make out what the swirls meant. But now I thought, 'He'll soon be here – are we ready?' The responsibility hit me hard. I went home and hugged everyone and told them I was going to be a great Mum!

The quality of the nurturance the baby receives in the womb in terms of oxygen, food and the efficient removal of waste products is critical too, for these affect the child's development in terms of strength and wellbeing. The mother's age is also important for young eggs are most fertile. Many studies show that the optimum time for childbearing is in the early twenties and that first-time mothers of thirty-five and over are twice as likely to have some pregnancy complication. Interestingly, middle-class women who have unusual increases in stress levels during pregnancy are identified as being susceptible to having babies of low birth weight while poor women who live with stress on a daily basis cope better. All of these are important socio-economic influences on how ready and able the mother and child will be to participate in the hazardous birth process without harm.

A worrying environmental hazard is the fact that diseases in the mother can affect the unborn child. Some drugs and viruses attack the placenta reducing the nutrients that pass to the baby. Others pass through the placental filters and attack the baby itself. Examples are rubella (German measles) particularly if this is caught in the first month of gestation. Then half the infants will have problems with sight and/or hearing loss. This is why most girls in the western world are routinely vaccinated. Cytomegalovirus (CMV) is less well known. This is a virus in the herpes group and is potentially the single most important infectious cause of mental retardation. And, of course, genital herpes in the mother can mean a caesarean birth is necessary. This in itself may cause primitive reflexes to be retained, causing difficulties with skills such as writing later on. So the quality of the earliest environment can have profound and long lasting implications for the intellectual, emotional and motor development of the unborn child.

At birth and soon after birth

At birth the baby is dependent on others for food, shelter, warmth and protection and so, even although the newborn will respond indiscriminately to parents or other caregivers at this stage, the earliest relationships are vitally important for survival. At only ten minutes old babies have been shown to be capable of mimicking pulled faces. To do this they show that they have some reflexive or instinctive reactions that help them bond socially with their parents. Parents instinctively welcome their child into the world with gentle rhythmic tones and the baby is soothed by the patterned sounds they hear. Babies are also alert to visual stimuli, such as things that move around and have contour stimulation (Smith *et al.* 2002). At birth, babies can see quite clearly at feeding distance, but beyond that things are hazy. This is because there was no light to stimulate the optic receptors in the womb, but very soon they are looking and learning and absorbing everything they see.

Recent research into autism, using gaze-tracking devices shows that babies on the autistic spectrum may have concentrated on the lower half of their parents' faces and so missed the messages that spring from eye contact (cited in Moore 2004). Does this explain at least part of the difficulty that these children have in holding eye contact later on? This sounds eminently feasible, but contradicting this possibility, Moore (2004) tells of her son George who, 'actively sought out eye contact'. From the start his eyes followed her around the room. At two or three days old, this baby boy became really distressed if she left his field of vision. Even the nurses commented, 'There's a boy who loves his Mum'. Yet later George was found to be severely autistic.

The babies' first cries are social messages too. They indicate that the baby is hungry or uncomfortable and mothers are primed to respond! It is *almost* impossible to ignore a crying baby. This interaction is called 'contingent responsiveness' and many studies have shown that that kind of maternal sensitivity leads to good social development in the infant. Many gifted and talented children will have shown a high level of awareness of how their behaviour can elicit the kind of responses they wish to have. In fact researchers, for example Bornstein and Sigman (1986), suggest that such infant alertness predicts much of the variation in intelligence in early childhood.

Many mothers of very lively, alert babies have described the earliest days at home as 'extremely tiring' because of babies 'hardly closing their eyes, demanding attention at all hours of the day and night'. Does this link to the extreme restlessness that often is present in gifted and talented children?

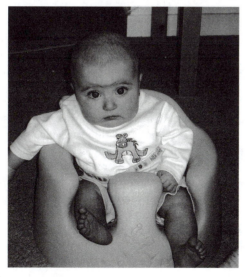

Figure 3.1   A very alert baby

These babies learn to control their environment very early and soon the home revolves around the child! So, even in the first months, babies are making social strides. They learn to discriminate their mother's voice from strangers' voices in the first few days and by six months they can discriminate between familiar and unfamiliar adults and adapt their interaction skills to suit.

Gifted and talented children also tend to be larger and stronger at birth. Given the anxiety that a fragile baby causes, the size as well as the alertness helps parents to relax and not transmit anxiety/stress to their child. Some advantaged parents of course have the resources to pay for someone to provide support and give them time to rest or socialise away from their child – important for recharging batteries!

Social influences in the home environment

The home environment includes such things as composition and financial status of the family (nuclear or single parent, with or without siblings, with or without support from relations, friends, support workers and the local community, advantaged in resource terms or struggling to survive). And in educational terms, whether the child's environment complements the school system in terms of expected behaviour, learning and conformity to rules is important too, because conflict can arise when ideas about what is best, differ!

Adopted children

The study of adopted children has been used to prove the effect of environment, because adopted children are not genetically related to the family who rear them. So researchers have selected these children to try to tease out the influences of inheritance (nature) and environment (nurture) on children's intelligence. This is extraordinarily difficult because of the multitude of variables (parenting skills, position of the child in the family, the health of the child preventing the same level of educational input) that interact and nullify claims. To make their results viable and reliable, early researchers studied identical twins and fraternal twins brought up separately and together. Their claims that because twins reared apart were found to have similar IQ scores, IQ was highly heritable, were criticised on the grounds that the numbers studied were low and 'being reared separately' was not adequately defined. If one adopted twin was brought up by a relative in close proximity to the family home, then interaction with the biological family was likely. This biased the research findings. But anecdotal stories of twins reared miles apart and only meeting in midlife must throw light on claims too. They have been found to be clones in appearance, in the jobs they do, in the families they have, in personal preferences for colours, even holidays and in many other aspects of their chosen lifestyle. Surely this can be regarded as 'evidence'?

Another variable to contaminate evidence is raised by Meadows (2002). She explains that because adoptive parents have to be 'suitable' and because they have had to go through many processes to prove this, they are usually highly motivated to nurture the child. This may detract from their 'being similar to the usual population of parents and prevent generalisation of the results.

Nonetheless the findings are noteworthy in that they show that adopted children, reared with parents with a higher IQ status than the biological parents and with the social and economic advantages they might not have had, show a higher IQ score than if they had been reared in their first home. This finding presents a strong case for the environment influencing intelligence. And so while the genetic inheritance determines potential, the environment influences how close children come to reaching it. It would seem that most gifted and talented children have the best of both worlds with both genetic and environmental advantages, and yet many would claim that children who have to strive to meet their goals – those who are intrinsically motivated enough to overcome disadvantages – can do very well. If they have to overcome hurdles but stay motivated and committed, they can achieve more than those who have the advantages but who lack the urge to succeed. 'The most important trait is diligence' (Hirsh 2007).

The interaction of the genotype and the phenotype

The genotype is a specific set of instructions contained in the gene pool while the phenotype is a product of three things. These are the genotype, the environment and the interaction of the first with the second. Bee (2004) explains that a child may have a genotype for a very high IQ, but if the mother has high alcohol consumption or takes drugs during pregnancy this could damage the nervous system to the extent that the child became retarded. Similarly a child could inherit genes for a difficult temperament, but sensitive interactions by the parents could reduce the negative effects. So the genotype sets out specific genetic codes, but the outcome is modified or enhanced by the kinds of experiences the child has from the moment of conception.

Temperament and personality: how do they contribute to high ability?

So, what kinds of backgrounds and experiences are going to promote the competences that put children into the talented bracket? The Centre for Longitudinal Studies at the University of London considered the attainment of 15,500 children and found that by the time they were three years old 'the offspring of graduate parents were ten months ahead of children of relatively unqualified parents in vocabulary, and a year ahead in their comprehension of sizes, shapes, colours and numbers'. This is a huge gap even before school begins.

Overcoming inequalities

Some children from Bangladeshi families, according to the aforementioned research, were 'a year behind white children in measurement of "school readiness"'. Perhaps these families had their own set of goals that were not amenable to measurement? However in trying to explain the gap, it was mooted that 'some immigrant mothers couldn't go out to work and so their children missed out on nursery education'. Perhaps they believed that home education would be best? After all their children might be bilingual and have great cultural awareness. The question as to whether these attributes were part of the test for school readiness is an interesting one. But, of course, if poverty is part of the equation, the families are unlikely to have the resources to stimulate the children. Books, trips and materials to encourage creativity may all be scarce or non-existent.

Another piece of research (Caplan *et al.* 1992) studied refugee families, 'who had experienced extreme hardship and had four or more children' – factors not usually associated with high achievement. This research produced very different results. These children all attended schools in low-income city-centre areas in the USA not often known for academic success. Yet a large number of these children did outstandingly well in their academic grades. While their grades in English were unexceptional, in science and maths almost half scored 'A' and a third of the remainder achieved 'B'. They scored well above the national average. Further study into how these children had achieved so well showed that although the families could not 'engage in the content of the homework, they collaborated in setting up 'homework stations' and study was given priority – it was a way of life. The older children helped the younger ones 'and in doing so relearned themselves'.

Another possible reason was that 'middle classes assimilate better all the warnings about junk food, smoking and spend more time communicating with their children. They also spend less time watching television and take part in sports, music and other activities of their choice' (Bee 2004). There have been longstanding claims that children with middle class backgrounds or well-educated parents as a rule do better throughout their educational careers and stay longer in education. Despite many interventions, the socio-economic status of the family is still a fairly good predictor of academic achievement. So if inequalities like this could be evened out, would there still be differences in children? Would more children from less advantaged homes feature in the gifted and talented categories? What are other things that make each one unique?

The influence of temperament

From the earliest days, babies vary in their behaviour. Some are placid while others are very active; some cry a lot and others are easy to settle and these characteristics, because they are inherited (Thomas and Chess 1977), do endure. They form the emotional core of the personality. In infancy characteristics such as 'typical activity level, irritability or soothability, fearfulness and sociability' are some of the identified descriptors. Those who support the view that temperament is seen in enduring individual differences in behaviour claim that the early demonstration is the matrix from which later child and adult personality develops. Many pieces of research have failed to agree on the list of characteristics that make up temperament. However, Thomas and Chess, perhaps the best known of the group, penned this trilogy.

Thomas and Chess (1977) typology of temperament

- *The easy child*: the easy child is regular in biological functioning with good sleeping and eating cycles. He is usually happy and adjusts easily to change.
- *The difficult child*: the difficult child is less regular in body functioning and is slow to develop sleeping and eating habits. He reacts negatively and vigorously to new things, is more irritable and cries more. His cries also have a more 'spoiled' grating sound than do the cries of 'easy' babies.
- *The slow-to-warm-up child*: this child shows few intense reactions, either positive or negative to new experiences. As a baby he may show a kind of passive resistance, such as drooling out unwanted new foods rather than spitting them out or crying. Once he has adapted to something new, however, his reaction is usually fairly positive.

Bee (2004) plots the characteristics on a continuum, showing that traits may be subtle or strident and vary depending on the circumstances the child has experienced and will face (Table 3.1).

But of course the environment plays a large part too. It is not difficult to understand how an irritable, fractious baby can make a new, weary mother despair, especially if family members imply that her parenting skills are to blame. The mother may even come to resent the baby especially if she lacks sleep and is not fully recovered from the birth. In fact another school of thought claims that temperamental characteristics are not innate but are responses to the early interactions between parents and child. This is an interesting argument. If temperament is inherited, then changing the environment and the caregiver should not change the child's behaviour, but if temperamental traits are caused by the environment, behaviour should alter. Bee's (2004) research claims that temperament is 'relatively enduring'. She finds that children, given explanations and role models, can learn to respond in different ways, but she also finds that when the context is new or stressful, children revert

Table 3.1 Characteristics continuum

Extrovert	⟷	Introvert
Vulnerable	⟷	Resilient
Excitable	⟷	Calm
Committed	⟷	Neglectful
Reluctant	⟷	Motivated
Obsessed	⟷	Laissez-faire
Irritable	⟷	Placid
Confident	⟷	Shy
Overactive	⟷	Passive
Distracted	⟷	Focussed
Withdrawn	⟷	Exuberant

to their inherited pattern of behaviour. While the discussions rage on, at least everyone agrees that temperamentally difficult babies and children are much more challenging to rear. Moreover, they seem to be more at risk for later behavioural problems (Meadows 2002). And as these characteristics are separate from intelligence, gifted and talented children show the same range of traits. What they may do is appreciate earlier that certain ways of behaving secure the outcome they want to have, but they may find it impossible to maintain this stance and revert to their innate way when they relax in the safety of their own home.

Temperament and environment

Although it is important to recognise the importance of temperament and how it influences children's behaviour and attitudes towards living and learning, the child's temperament does not inevitably determine personality.

These early characteristics do affect relationships and these are not one-sided exchanges. The baby is gradually learning to evaluate how others respond and building up a picture of his own self-worth. This is the earliest burgeoning of the self-concept that houses the self-esteem.

The self-concept and the self-esteem

Most practitioners would agree that nurturing each child's self-esteem is a key aspect of their teaching, because if children are confident in themselves they are more likely to make friends, explain their wishes and want to learn new things. The self-esteem is the evaluative part of the self-concept.

The self-concept

The self-concept is the name given to the picture children build of themselves as time goes by. So observations such as, 'I am a boy with fair hair; I am tall and enjoy music; I have two sisters who like to read books; my Dad is a fisherman' and so on, all contribute to the self-concept. But as awareness of the social context grows and children meet in groups each child begins to evaluate the characteristics he thinks he has against those he would like to have and those he thinks his friends have. He compares his own self to his ideal self. The difference between the two is important. If the child thinks he can close the gap, then he may well strive to make this happen, but if the gap is too large and closing it is felt to be unrealistic, then this is harder to accept. The interesting thing is that the child's self-evaluation may not be accurate in someone else's eyes.

The self-esteem

The formation of the self-esteem is an interactive process, often called 'a tridimensional image' or 'a looking-glass self'. The children read other people's reactions and evaluate these as being positive or negative. This gives rise to the saying, 'What I think of myself depends on what I think others think of me!' Again, the children's evaluations may not be accurate. But because what they perceive to be correct has such an influence on their self-perception and resultant behaviour, practitioners strive to interact with each child in a consistent, positive way. This is harder than it appears because the children constantly judge their own efforts too, and as they mature they can make sophisticated assessments as to their success. Being told they are good at something when they know perfectly well that this is not true is not helpful and only demeans the assessor in the child's eyes. This shows how the self-evaluation is constrained by the credibility the child gives to the assessor.

At first sight, many people would consider that gifted and talented children must have a high self-esteem and in many cases this is so. But other children, finding their gift or talent makes them different from their peers can actually take steps to hide or deny its existence. They will take steps to underachieve. Of course this depends on what the gift or talent is and how other children value it. If their talent is sports- or music-based then that is rarely spurned, but a talent in maths or language – the very attributes most schools seek to promote – may well be jettisoned to the despair of parents and professionals alike.

Parenting skills: to what extent are parenting styles important in developing gifts and talents?

One of the most hotly debated issues in relation to the nurturance of gifted and talented children is the part parents play. Scarr's (2002) research plays down the importance of parenting styles beyond 'minimum or good enough parenting'. She claims that parents 'need only provide a basically warm, supportive and nurturing environment for their children to develop their innate potential to the full'. She claims that the family environment beyond these basic needs is of little importance. This is backed up by her findings that children reared in the same family show little similarity as they grow up. If this is so, then individual differences are largely down to heredity, not environment. She claims that gifted and talented children 'are born with something extra that their upbringing can't explain'. Sroufe and his colleagues (1990) completed a longitudinal study to find if securely attached infants became confident youngsters at 11 years. They found that children who had early secure attachments with their parents were more self-confident and had more sympathetic interactive skills; they had more friends and were likely to be chosen as leaders. They expressed more positive emotions and were more likely to engage in complex actions. They had a greater sense of being able to accomplish things. These findings point to a long-term influence of early positive parental interactions. This backs up the importance of the social environment on development.

But what kind of parental input stimulates children to be confident, approachable, non-aggressive learners? Can parental affection buffer children against other kinds of disadvantage? Melby and Conger (1996) say 'yes'. They found that maternal affection was the key to promoting positive behaviour and achievement in children. If this is combined with high expectations or maturity demands, then children are empowered to do well.

Bee (2004) in her study of parenting styles considers three main types. These are:

- the permissive parental style that is high in nurturing but low in maturity demands;
- the authoritarian style that is high in control and maturity demands but low in nurturance; and
- communication and the authoritative parenting style that is high in all four.

The most consistently high outcomes link to the authoritative style where there is a balance in providing guidance and allowing freedom for the children to make decisions and eventually to follow their own wishes.

Parents of gifted and talented children often or even always have to make adjustments and even sacrifices to their normal family routine. Supporting a child with a gift or talent is both expensive and time-consuming, especially if extra training happens far from home. Given these inputs it can be hard for parents not to put unrealistic expectations on their children or resent waning interest when children do not fulfil their potential. For while opportunity makes a critical difference, the children themselves shape their future.

Different childcare practices: do they influence development?

The environment beyond the parental home is of immense importance to parents. Until relatively recently the expectation was that most mothers would stay at home to care for their children until school age. Any nursery time was most often seen as a social gathering where children could make friends. Nursery education was not given the high educational priority it has today. In 2008, however, many more families, for career or financial reasons, require childcare support. Sometimes grandparents help out because of preference or because childcare places are limited. There are around 80,000 home-based childminders who are registered in the UK, ensuring a level of competence, but many more care for children on an informal basis.

Comparing and contrasting the effects of the different ways is complex because so many variables impinge, such as the quality of the care that is given, the adaptability of the child in a strange situation, and the length of time the child is away from the parent. This explains why research results conflict. In Sweden the authorities have responded to the finding that childcare in the first year could be detrimental to relationships between parents and their child by allowing parents to take a year off work on full pay! Very often the mother will take the first nine months and the father the later three months. (Hwang *et al.* 1990). In the absence of such generosity, parents in the UK have to make arrangements much earlier. Melluish (1990) compared the progress of nine-month-old children who experienced care with relatives, childminding, or private nursery care. Obviously the child:adult ratio was different. At 18 months the communication aspects of development were highest for children cared for by relatives and lowest in the nursery group, however the nursery scored best in fostering prosocial behaviour such as sharing and caring. There were no significant differences in cognitive development and no detriment in the relationships between the children and their parents and this finding held across social groups.

Studies of gifted and talented children in the Key Stage 2 (Primary 3 and 4) years show that the school environment can make a huge difference to the child. As the borderline between gifted and talented children and the others is not clearly defined, children can be overlooked and, in extreme cases, their frustration can cause them to be seen as aggressive troublemakers. One child, Ian, hated school and was so disruptive that he was referred to a special school for disturbed children. Testing by an educational psychologist found that he had an IQ of 170. He had the mental age of an 18-year-old yet had to stay with the school curriculum for 9-year-olds.

In her earlier research, Freeman (1980) found that such frustration came not only from the giftedness but also from parental pressures. The parents of gifted children were more likely to be dissatisfied with the school and the children picked up on this. The parents were also likely to put a great deal of pressure on their children to achieve, possibly because, even despite their professional status, they were dissatisfied with the hand life had dealt them. So environmental influences on gifted and talented children are hard to measure. It is hoped that the new emphasis on parental/professional relationships will enable full and frank discussions so that all the parties concerned learn from each other, respect each others' views and share strategies to support their gifted and talented children. This is the best way to nurture respect, relationships and responsive care.

Chapter 4

Practical activities to intrigue gifted and talented children at school

The activities in this chapter have all been tried out in primary schools and nursery/foundation stage settings. Some topics have been instigated by teachers and nursery nurses, and the children have developed them with often surprising results; others have been stimulated by children's drawings or ideas raised in chats and discussions. Sometimes older children passing by the developing project have brought in extra resources – for instance, in the bear scenario one child brought in pictures of koala bears and a piece of bamboo – and some have negotiated time to make or search for props. In all of the activities the purpose is to encourage logical thought through problem solving and creative/imaginative thinking. This is to stimulate the frontal cortex of the brain. The children also learn to listen to each other and treat ideas with respect.

Some of the ideas could be regarded as 'fillers', e.g. the sudoku, suggested to keep early finishers absorbed, but even then there are different levels of difficulty so that the most able are challenged. Sudoku is an activity that requires logical reasoning yet can be completed quite quickly, so it is purposeful and satisfying for the children. Other suggestions are whole group, longer-term activities that develop as the experience goes on. The topic named 'putting on a show', started as a nursery corner idea after one gifted four-year-old made a programme replicating one she had bought in a real theatre. But the idea blossomed, parents got involved and all the different parts of the production kept volunteer children from different classes busily learning over a whole term. 'Cinderella' was produced as a fundraiser at Christmas and a small donation was sent to the local special needs school.

Some ideas were borrowed from other people for example, 'the six thinking hats' from Edward De Bono and 'the importance of fantasy play' from Vivian Gussin Paley. These have been acknowledged, briefly explained and the original source has been given in the bibliography, so that those who wish to follow the ideas through can find the source material.

In all the activities the aim is to leave ownership of the development and outcome with the children with the clear understanding that all who wish must be able to join in. To follow the children successfully, however, practitioners have to have the required level of background knowledge or be able to suggest resources that will take the play forward. In this way the adults become facilitators. In nurturing gifted and talented children this can be very demanding, especially if the activity develops into the children's particular areas of expertise. It can also be hard for teachers to decide if an activity has usefully run its course and should finish (although children in the nursery soon show their interest has waned by wandering off) or if their intervention will cut down the creative thinking that was just about to emerge!

Some of the suggested activities will be directly applicable in any setting with any age group. Others need amending to suit different children. Very often, the amendment can be in the way the topic is approached and discussed rather than changing the activity itself. Alternatively practitioners might prefer to think of revitalising the content they are familiar with by turning it into a problem solving exercise. That can add a different kind of challenge and allow the children to think creatively. This is hard to do but is the essence of a child-centred curriculum.

After each example links to curricular documents are given. This shows how the aims can be fulfilled through enjoyable activities. Children of all abilities can make their contribution. Respectful listening develops too.

Example 1: Conservation/recycling

Many children have environmentally friendly parents at home and are adept at knowing where to save their different kinds of waste. They are probably aware of how savings in energy can be made. So an initial discussion of why they are recycling (because the landfill sites are full and the planet needs to be saved from overusage of non-sustainable fuels) might lead to the children considering the life of the men who work on the landfill sites.

The following example of the interaction following the discussion was taped to show the kind of responses that could be given. The teacher/practitioners' input is 'T' and a selection of the children's responses 'C.' Those made by the most able are marked *

T: As they take their diggers into the mire, what might they turn up? (If the children aren't used to discussions it's a good idea to make a list of possible things in case the children don't offer many suggestions.)

C: Tin cans: Some people don't wash them out and the gulls feed on the bits that are left in.

C*: Not enough to save our depleted fish stocks especially haddock – we have to eat cod now. When you go to the Bass Rock and see hundreds of birds it shows how much fish is lost.

C*: Dead bodies without heads on! We could make up a graveyard story, but if there was no head who would come to the cemetery? How would we know who it was?

C: How would a body get to the infill site?

C*: I know – helicopters would drop them – so if you want to find out who did the murder ask the police for names of everyone who has a helicopter.

C: What should the men at the site do? I think they should just cover it over for you couldn't find who did it anyway.

T: If people were better at recycling, would this help? When you recycle the waste gets made into something else. What do you think of that?

C*: If tin cans have to be taken to a factory, that takes energy too. I don't think anyone has researched the costs – it might be easier just to explode the rubbish on the site.

T: Are there any other down sides to recycling? Would you like to work on a landfill site?

C: Well it could be like a treasure hunt if there were jewels and precious things there, but not if there were just old cans, no thanks!

C: Not me, I'm not going to wear clothes made out of dirty junk, are you?

Once a topic like this has been raised by the children or instigated by the practitioners as part of a local initiative perhaps, then the mode of interaction is important. The change comes in reformulating questions as statements or shared experiences. This is difficult but it can produce longer, more thoughtful replies that produce a deeper level of thinking.

Example 2: The same topic with five-year-olds

T: I know a man who works on a landfill site and he can hardly cope with all the rubbish coming in. He says there is always a bad smell (showing a picture of a landfill site with seagulls swooping overhead).

C: We go to the tip and we have to put all the stuff in separate bins and then it goes away in big lorries. Dad takes bags of rubbish, stuff from the garden and old teles and things. The tip is very tidy but the men are as grumpy as anything.

C*: What makes it smell then? I think there's a dead person buried there. Or a dead fox. My mum says it's dangerous for our cat because the foxes come into the gardens looking for food now. That's because we have wheely bins. So we feed the foxes and keep our cat inside after dark.

C*:   It's all the stuff rotting, that's why the gulls are swooping down. I once was at the beach and a huge gull came down to steal our picnic. They are huge birds and always hungry because they fly away over the sea.

From a tiny beginning the children have raised so many issues that can be developed by practitioners who listen and pick up the cues. Interrupting by asking questions or not giving the children time to think can spoil the flow of ideas, but practitioners have to be ready with ideas of their own in case the children stay silent.

Example 3: Avoiding questions in discussing the story of 'The three little pigs'

T: I think the three little pigs would be very sad to leave home.
C*:   No they wouldn't because there were new piglets and there was no room left in the house.
C: I've got a new baby and he takes up too much room in my bedroom. I wish I could go and build a house in the garden and he could live there.
C: A baby is not the same as piglets. There's only one baby and lots of pigs.
C: How many piglets were there? I think wee pink pigs look lovely
T: I think your Mum would cry if you left home. I think the pigs' mum felt like that.
C*:   If she was a kind mum they wouldn't go far away – just up the hill a bit because they had to carry the stuff to build the house. Maybe that's why one of them used straw, much lighter than carrying hods of bricks.
C: When you grow up you get a house anyway. When my brother got a flat Mum said it was peaceful now. She wouldn't have to put up with the loud music any more.
C*:   We need to win the lottery to buy a house now. I expect we'll live at home forever because there aren't many good jobs that pay enough. I think I'll live on a farm and build a house of straw … and I'll make friends with the wolf and feed him and he won't want to eat me any more.

It is much harder to follow the children's ideas and not to dictate the sequence of events especially when they wander from the original plan, but this strategy provides insights into children's thinking and helps keep the development child-friendly.

EYFS (Early Years Foundation Stage) goals: interact with others; negotiating plans: find out about their environment and talk about the features they like and dislike.
SCE (Scottish Curriculum for Excellence) goals: discuss and evaluate environmental issues.

Creative thinking: make your body better

The original idea is from De Bono's work on lateral thinking. Children of all ages enjoy this challenge. The older ones can draw the improved version then discuss the pros and cons of the changes. After time to try they can vote on the change they would all enjoy.

EYFS goals: extending opportunities for creativity; finding out about living things.
SCE goals: thinking creatively; openness to new ideas; making reasoned evaluations.

Shared ideas from children (3–11)

The teacher drew the 'improvements' for a group of nursery children. The older children did this as a small group activity with one child adding the suggestions. Eventually the whole class did lifesize drawings of themselves with their own improvements added and discussed both the advantages and disadvantages of their plan!

The children had great fun suggesting these ideas. Then they had to choose one and think of the advantages and disadvantages of making the alteration! Suggestions were:

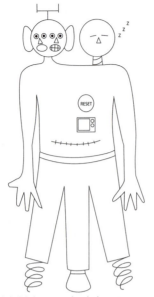

1 Have two heads so that we can sleep during maths

2 Have an aerial to pick up football scores

3 Have a zip to let the baby out

4 Have huge hands to be a good goalie

5 Have spings to bounce to school

6 Have teeth that never get bad

7 Have trousers that grew with your feet

Figure 4.1 Make your body better

- If you had eyes all round your head you would need lots of specs and how would you fit them on? But it would be good at a football match because you could see the whole pitch and both goals at once.
- If you had springs for feet, Mum wouldn't let you walk on the wood floors but it would be worth it to be a good goalie. And think how fast you could run!
- I think a reset button would keep us all healthy. It would save the health service millions of pounds and no one would die. So we wouldn't need a heaven would we?

The children then voted for the best idea. They were unanimous in voting that the bonus of not having to visit a dentist was best! Only one child could think of disadvantages of that. His father was a dentist!

Sudoku

Sudoku is a game of logic, not maths. For children who enjoy numbers, Sudoku using numbers up to 5 can be fun. Gifted children can be given a blank grid and make their own challenges for the other children or practitioners to try!

1	2		5	
2	3		5	
	4		1	2
4		1		3
5		2	3	

This is a complete grid using numbers up to 6. All the children can play. Just remove more for the gifted ones to challenge their thinking.

1	3	6	4	5	2
2	1	5	3	4	6
3	4	1	6	2	5
6	5	4	2	3	1
4	6	2	5	1	3
5	2	3	1	6	4

An interesting variation for children who don't yet recognise numbers or who are put off by thinking this is a mathematical activity when in truth it is a logical challenge, is to substitute pictures for numbers. Children can make patterns even if they do not play the full game. There is a sudoku board made of coloured patterns on the market which is advertised in various Early Years catalogues. Using this grid, children who are not ready to tackle the game can sort colours together and develop their fine motor skills replacing the cubes in the boxes and making paths (e.g. the yellow brick road.) This board can be used for sorting and matching colours and for making patterns as well as for the intended game.

Developing awareness of the importance of number in the children's environment

T: I wonder what numbers really are?

C*: Signs that tell us how many things there are.

C: I see numbers at the snack table, beside the aprons, when we make shopping lists and when we work in the café and the shop.

T: Let's think of where else we see numbers.

C: Petrol filling stations, bus stops, prices in shops, on lampposts, manhole covers; on the front of the bus; on road signs telling you how fast you can go; at the airport telling you how much to pay, dialling the telephone, the lottery!

T: Let's think of birthday numbers.

C: We'll make a bar graph and every time someone has a birthday they can alter the pattern. How's that?

Responses from children 6–9

T: I wonder if there are games where you have to count using your numbers?

C: Snakes and ladders, ludo, chess, dominoes, jigsaws.

C*: You have to keep the score at tennis or football so that's about numbers; scientists read graphs and cartographers read maps. Then all those who navigate airships and pilots who take ships through canals have to know the measurements of their ship so they need to understand numbers too.

T: Let's think of when we count when we make things such as making a necklace of beads or straws at the threading table. (Look at different patterns and explain how balance in the pattern can be achieved. Older children could look at and then make Viking jewellery). Are there other activities where you do counting?

C: Five little buns in a baker's shop, building bricks, checking to see how many people are at the snack table, looking at the clock to see when it's time to go home.

The gifted children can make bar charts of children's heights; pie charts of children's preferences such as the games they like to play, or they can do small pieces of market research finding out where parents like to shop and how prices compare.

EYFS goals: recognise numerals; use developing mathematical ideas to solve problems.
SCE goals: make reasoned evaluations; use numeracy skills.

Developing mathematical vocabulary through activities

This is an activity to develop problem solving and creative thinking in the nursery/reception classes.

Teddy Bear

This idea was led by a child who was fascinated by Paddington Bear.

Stimulus: Find an abandoned teddy or puppet in the garden with the words 'Help Me Please' on a card tied onto his coat.

Discussion topics

T: I had a teddy when I was small – he was my favourite toy (stimulating discussion on the children's favourite).

T: I wonder where this teddy came from? (have pictures of aliens, planets available to follow up suggestions the children make).

T: I think he has he been there since yesterday (discussion of state of clothes or dirty face).

T: I wonder if (the janitor, the secretary or the lollipop lady) saw him this morning? (bringing another person into the discussion and encouraging reflection and discussion about the early start others have to get the setting prepared for the day).

T: What can we do to make him feel better? Can anyone think of a good name for this teddy? (If none forthcoming: would 'Marmalade' be a good one? (discussion of why and why not).

Table 4.1 Mathematical vocabulary

Run over and pass	BETWEEN	the skittles
Stretch out	SIDEWAYS	to grasp the pole
Stand over there	OPPOSITE	your partner
Put your foot on the	EDGE	of the circle
Make a	ZIG ZAG	pattern on the floor
Follow closely	BEHIND	your leader
Move one foot over to the	LEFT/RIGHT	and bring it back again
	CROSS OVER	to the other side
Run/walk/stroll	FORWARDS	
	BACKWARDS	
	DIAGONALLY	
	AROUND	the hoops

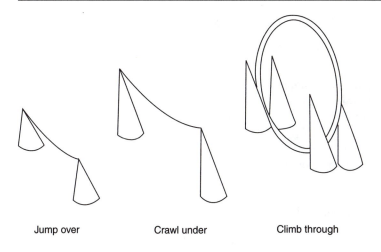

Jump over   Crawl under   Climb through

Add several hoops to crawl through

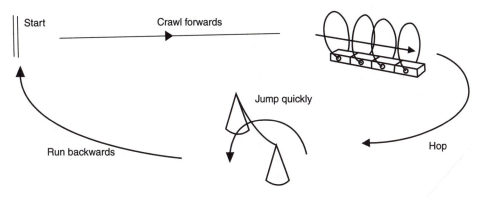

Figure 4.2 Directions exercise

T: Do you think we could give him a good home? Where he would like his house to be? He might like to swim or climb trees? (these pointers can lead to a discussion of what makes a good home for a Bear or what ever the puppet is).

Linked activities

- Choosing a friend for the bear from the toy box. Ask the children to explain their selection and to make up a game for them to play together. (This could be a ball game or it could involve talking about friendships and the qualities children look for when making a friend).
- The children have to explain their game to the toy. This is easier than speaking out loud in front of classmates. If bullying is an issue, for often gifted children can be bullied, then the toys can act out the characteristics of a bully and a victim so driving home social messages without naming any children.
- Writing/posting/emailing letters to invite other toys to the bear's birthday party.
- Making up stories, poetry, tongue twisters, songs. Record these on tape can be a meaningful use of technology as well as letting the children hear their efforts.

One example of a poem written by a gifted seven-year-old is:

Marmalade
My little bear has two big eyes.
We found him in the garden. What a surprise!
He wasn't in the garden yesterday,
So where did he come from?
He won't say!

We've built him a house in a sunny spot
He likes to sleep there –
He goes there quite a lot
But when we're quiet he comes out to play
And we share our snack so he won't run away.

We called him Marmalade
'Cos his coat is brown
We've made him a tie, so
He's the smartest bear in town.

He's found a new friend who was lonely and sad
And now they're together. We are so glad
For it's good to have friends and we're all friends here,
So come and visit us before the end of the year!

This idea was developed into dramatic role-play so all the children tried moving like bears (big crawling actions), they pretended to pick up objects with paws and carry them home. Still crawling on all fours, they hid behind trees, growled and enjoyed 'fun wrestling' (growling and making menacing moves with no contact allowed) just like bear cubs do.

Resources to encourage further study

Factual books about polar bears/brown bears/koala bears in their very different environments.

After individual study, older children could discuss the availability of bamboo and how the sources of this food are dwindling. What can be done?

Activity: The teddy bears picnic for little ones; older children can make a collage of the bears in their very different environments and discuss their habitats and habits.

The youngest children can bring in their own teddies or favourite toys and have a teddy bears picnic. They love to sing the song and can act out the stealthy creeping of the children who go down to the woods. They can have their snack outdoors when the outdoor area has become a picnic spot.

EYFS goals: identify features of living things/objects they observe.
SCE goals: develop ethical views; apply critical thinking in new contexts.

Pattern and shape identification helping literacy

T: Everyone make a line behind Jack (teacher takes Jack's hand and leads round to form a circle).

T: Take hands facing inwards – let's make the circle bigger and smaller. Let's think of stretchy words (pull, grow, swell, puff out) and squashy words (shrink, narrow, close in, collapse like a balloon when pricked by a pin).

Developments

How many steps to the centre of the circle? The children can try out giant steps and fairy steps, heel to toe steps and tiptoe steps, noisy steps and quiet steps.

EYFS goals: describe the sizes and shapes: recognise simple patterns.
SCE goals: learn independently and as part of a group.

Activities to develop visual-spatial intelligence in older children

- Movement activities emphasising direction e.g. keeping parallel with a partner while marching; running diagonally to the corner of the room
- Making diagrams/maps
- Designing a room with furniture
- Tessellation and patterns (handling tiles and fitting them together to make a roof.)
- Craft and art work
- Making images in 3D.

EYFS goals: describe the sizes and shapes: recognise simple patterns.
SCE goals: use technology for learning.

Activities to develop body/kinaesthetic intelligence

Body/kinaesthetic intelligence is typically found in those who have a high control over their movements, for example ballet dancers, athletes, gymnasts, surgeons.

- All forms of movement to develop fine, gross and manipulative skills
- Crossing the midline activities e.g. using twirling ribbons to make figures of eight; to draw the first letter of their names, to draw shapes in the air and in the sand
- Hand/kicking dominance activities e.g. throwing and kicking
- Construction and 3D activities
- Drama
- Body awareness activities e.g. 'Simon says'

Developing literacy and movement for gifted and talented children

Resources: a large cardboard clock face made from cardboard with arrows for hands; laminated cards of action words e.g crumple, pop. Fix the words round the clockface.
   Teaching idea: The children use the arrows to choose actions and then build them into a movement sequence, e.g.

- dash and freeze, crumple and pop
- rush and explode, wither and die
- swivel and twist, uncurl and fly.

The children demonstrate the movement sequence to a friend who has to guess which words have been chosen. Then in twos they make up a four-word sequence together using contrasting words. They then use the space in the hall to:

   Dash from the corner to meet a friend in the centre of the space; freeze in a high jagged shape; slowly crumple together to the ground; then pop, pop, pop back to the corner.

Table 4.2 Action words

Travelling words	Dart, scamper, zip, plod, prowl, crawl, skip, rush, zoom fly dash
Jumping words	Leap, explode, fly, pounce, toss, pop, hop, bound
Gesturing words	Twist, gather, flop, crumple, jab, slice, point
Stillness words	Pause, hold, rest, die, linger, freeze, sleep

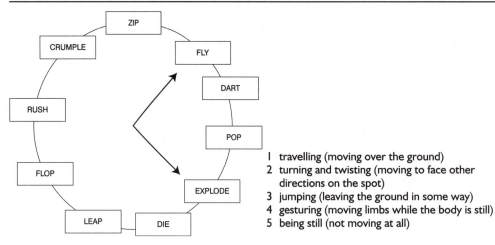

1 travelling (moving over the ground)
2 turning and twisting (moving to face other directions on the spot)
3 jumping (leaving the ground in some way)
4 gesturing (moving limbs while the body is still)
5 being still (not moving at all)

The children can use percussion instruments to accompany the movement and discuss the expressive qualities of both, for example, the Indian bells' prolonged sound is a good accompaniment to prowling.

Additional directional help may be necessary, for example 'Perhaps you would like to start apart and rush to meet as your partner in the centre of the room' or if the activity develops into group work 'begin close together in a group and spread out, then rush in again one by one to make a jagged shape like an iceberg. Melt slowly into the ground then spring away again'.

A reminder that 'everyone need not begin or finish at once' or the actions can be done in a round (after singing 'London's Burning' in a round to establish the idea) can add variety and stimulate a high level of listening and concentration. Once the children have established a sequence, then they can show the other children who have to guess what actions and directions they were demonstrating. In this way, all the children are involved in learning about words and understanding their meaning through trying them out.

Every action can fit into one of five categories (see Figure above). These basic actions can be developed by introducing descriptive words, helping literacy. Able children can analyse what the words mean and discuss how they can build contrasting words into a rhythmical movement sequence.

Many movement lessons can be made linking contrasting action words, e.g.:

- whirl and rest, creep and pounce
- stalk and pounce, crumple and shoot
- dash and explode, crumple and pop.

The quality of the movement is suggested by the words and should stimulate discussion, for example how does linger differ from the rest? The children can show as well as explain!

Introducing large apparatus

Large apparatus adds challenge to the development of gross motor skills. Apparatus can be arranged in a circuit to ease assessment or be rearranged by the children to give problem-solving opportunities.

Obviously this needs careful supervision, but it is a challenging activity that strengthens the body and gives confidence as well as competence. The apparatus should offer different levels of challenge to suit the abilities of all the children. Able children can rearrange apparatus to allow them to demonstrate action word sequences, for example, balance and swing, crawl and climb.

As apparatus arrangements are planned, it is critical that the kind of movements that are possible should be considered. This is important to get variety but also to consider safety – if it is possible that a child could run down or slide down an inclined bench, then enough space for that to happen safely must be part of the plan. The approach runs to different pieces of apparatus should not cut across one another. Thick mats are essential to pad falls and it goes without saying that the different pieces of apparatus should be splinter proof and secure.

Rules

Teachers may wish to consider whether it is necessary to have rules, e.g. only four children on the climbing frame at once. This will largely depend on the children and the number of adults who are able to supervise. If some children are put off by others being too close to them, then special arrangements or rules may be beneficial.

Better introducing the jingle?

A jingle can be a fun way to introduce separate pieces of apparatus gradually without losing all the sound teaching that has gone before.

EYFS goals: Move with confidence and safety.
SCE goals: Assess risk and make informed decisions.

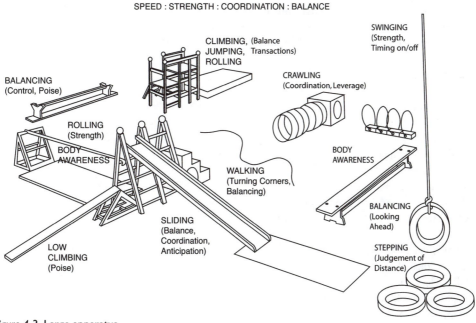

Figure 4.3 Large apparatus

Table 4.3 Appartus activities

Jingle	Helps	Teacher check
Walk along the bench	Balance, body awareness	Sense of security – wobbling, extra arm curling, arms flailing
Stretch tall, tall, tall	Poised walking	Emphasise head up if stretching arms is too difficult
Jump to the floor	Transfer of weight to different level	'Bendy' knees helping control – preventing jarring
Curl small, small, small	Body awareness (backs, head tucked in)	Round back (a practice for rolling); willingness to tuck head in
Slowly stretch out to the side (rising to standing)	Awareness of laterality	Check body stays erect and balanced as arms move
Push your fingers out so wide	Spatial awareness; distance from next child or wall	Can the arms be extended equally without looking or is the trunk twisted?
Whirl them round into a spin	Control and balance	Watch foot action. Pivoting, quick stepping or twisting and falling
Bend your elbows, pull them in	Sequential movement	Check elbows coming into sides to make two distinct movements
Stand tall	Regain balanced position	

Activities to develop musical intelligence

Musical intelligence is typically found in those able to convert sounds into rhythmical passages in music or poetry/writings:

- Using chants and raps to instil rhythmical awareness
- Playing musical instruments
- Making percussive instruments
- Recognising sounds in the environment
- All kinds of listening activities
- Repeating rhythmical clapping/tapping.

Tap time
Verse 1
Tap on your head
And clap, clap, clap
Tap on your knees
And flap, flap, flap
Look all around you
Who do you see?
Wave to them and join two hands
One, two, three

Verse 2: in twos facing a partner
Tap on their shoulders
Clap, clap, clap
Tap on their elbows
Flap, flap, flap

Look all around you
Who do you see?
Join up in a circle
One, two, three

Verse 3: in a circle facing the centre
Sit down in your circle
Clap, clap, clap
Wiggle all your toes around
Flap, flap, flap
Jump up to your feet again,
One two three
Make your circle spin around and then come back to me all come back to me!

EYFS goals: move with confidence and safety.
SCE goals: respect for others through fun activities emphasising rhythm and musicality.

Activities to develop interpersonal–intrapersonal or emotional intelligence

Interpersonal–intrapersonal or emotional intelligence is typically shown in situations where children show they understand the feelings of others. Socially able children are able to read non-verbal cues, but many gifted ones have difficulties.

Activity: Show the children pictures of other children displaying different emotions.

T: How do you think this boy is feeling? How do you know? Why does he feel like that do you think? How did you know he was sad/happy/angry? What could we do to help?

- Puppet stories depicting instances of bullying and helping the children understand why this is unacceptable.
- Giving positive feedback and helping children understand that they can encourage other children by giving them support.
- Self-esteem activities e.g. making lists of what the children consider what they do well for even gifted and talented children may not appreciate or value the abilities they have.
- Group discussions and projects e.g. evaluating current developments, e.g. 'Do wind farms do what they say? How could we find out?'
- Buddies – e.g. having the able children work with those who would welcome support.
- Making children aware of less fortunate others through films of children in the Third World.

EYFS goals: be sensitive to the needs and feelings of others.
SCE goals: respect different cultures through appreciating their cultural values.

Listening to tapes of different languages

Select a tape and picture book containing words and pictures in another language, perhaps one that is the home language of another child in the setting. The early years is a critical time for learning languages and the able child may well be intrigued. Children's DVDs in that language can offer further stimulation.

Older gifted and talented children can try to make up a new secret language of their own or they can learn the DEAF alphabet or even try to pass messages to each other in morse or semaphore.

EYFS goals: appreciating different ways of communicating.
SCE goals: learning about technology.

Six Thinking Hats

Resources: hats made of coloured card stapled to form a circle. There should be enough of each colour for the whole group either to wear the same colour or to change hats when the blue hat, the one in charge says so!

This is Edward de Bono's idea of a way to help children clarify their thinking (see de Bono's *Six Thinking Hats* in the bibliography).

They are given a 'problem' and then their answers or solutions must 'fit' the colour of hat that they wear. This saves them trying to consider every aspect of a possible solution at once and also asks them to concentrate on one kind of reply. If a child makes an incorrect response, the Blue Hat can reply, 'Woops, wrong hat!' This is a fun way of directing thinking – one that doesn't cause hurt. This strategy can be used with any age group either to recap on a story or to introduce discussions and debates.

The Blue Hat is a controlling hat, usually worn by the teacher until the children are familiar with the strategy. Then a child can take over. The person who wears the blue hat leads the activity and controls the timing of changing hats. Changing the hat alters the focus of a discussion ('Well we've thought of all the good things, now put on your black hats and think of disadvantages or things that we have to be careful about').

The White Hat focuses on information or facts. The children do not give their own opinions when wearing this hat. They are recapping, e.g. 'What does the story tell us?' 'What is the problem that we have to solve?'

The Yellow Hat is a sunny, positive hat. When the children wear this hat, they only think of the happy fortunate things that could happen. They think of possible happy outcomes if the problem is solved in this way.

The Red Hat asks the children to think of the feelings and emotions experienced by the characters. They might extend this to thinking about their own feelings just depending on what the problem is. So the question might be, 'How does that make you feel?' or 'In the story how did the (character) feel?'

The Green Hat is a creative hat when the children are asked to consider or invent different solutions to the problem. The questions, 'What else could we do?' or 'What other ways could we try?' would be appropriate here.

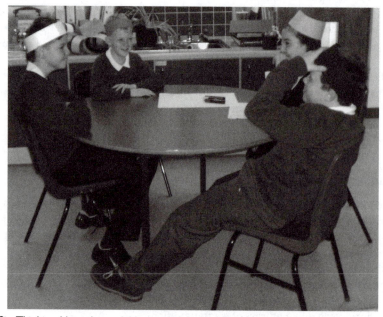

Figure 4.4 Six Thinking Hats: these children are debating the pros and cos of a school trip or a theatre visit

The Black Hat is the hat that urges caution. 'What difficulties might we find if we tried that?' or 'Do you think that would work? or 'Would there be danger in trying that?' are the kinds of interjections that could be appropriate when black hats are worn.

At the start, all the children would wear the same colour of hat. Then once the idea was assimilated, different groups could wear different colours and then come together to discuss the results.

Example

Once the children were familiar with a story, they could analyse the content in this way.

T;   Let's think of the Billy Goats Gruff trying to cross the bridge.
BLUE HAT: Put your green hats on and think of best ways the goats might try to get the fresh grass.
C: The should use a hot-air balloon and travel in the basket over to the grass.
BLUE HAT: Put your black hats on: What would the goats have to think about before they ventured across?
C: They might not be able to control the balloon – the wind could take them over the seas. How would they get home?

Or for older children nearing transition time

BLUE HAT: Put your yellow hats on and tell me all the good things that will happen when you go to the big class.
BLUE HAT: Has anybody got black hat worries? Let's see if we can use our green hats to make worries go away."

Gifted/older children might organise a debate, one group with black hats on to think of the difficulties that might happen when, for example, a fair came to town, while at the same time another group with yellow hats might think of the benefits to the area. At the same time the red hats might consider the feelings of the people who live near the fairground and the feelings of the people who run the fair.

This is a strategy that may have to be introduced one hat at a time but the children respond very positively and there is no doubt they are challenged to think about different possibilities.

EYFS goals: to listen to each other in a group.
SCE goals: To recognise that different people have different valid views.

Producing 'Cinderella' using the Six Thinking Hats approach

A four-year-old gifted child at nursery produced this programme after the group had visited a puppet theatre to see 'Jack and the Beanstalk'. The children were so excited and decided they could act out a play too. They decided to adopt Catriona's programme as a stimulus and began to consider all the elements of putting on a show.

Discussions were tried out using the Six Thinking Hats approach because the initial idea produced such a clamour; from 'I want to be Cinderella' to 'There's no pumpkins in the shops just now!' An extract from the issues raised follows.

TEACHER WITH BLUE HAT: We have decided to put on a play called 'Cinderella'. Everyone put on your white hats. Can everyone remember the story?
WHITE HATS   Who would come to our show?
Where would it be held?
Would everyone want to be in it?

Figure 4.5 The 'Cinderella' programme

	We'd have to organise it so that there were different jobs and have someone to check that everyone was able to do their job in time.
	What jobs would there be?
BLUE HAT	We could make a list and ask everyone what they would like to do. Put on your Yellow Hats and think of all the good things about putting on a play.
YELLOW HATS	It would be fun and let everyone know what we could do.
	We could work at different things – I'd like to paint the scenery.
	People could come and watch – maybe we could sell tickets and give the money to poor children.

	We could get party dresses and have a ball.
	We could make cakes and sell necklaces and our clay bowls with flowers in.
BLUE HAT	Would it be difficult to do a play like this? Could we manage do you think. Put your Black Hats on and tell me what sorts of things might be tricky?
BLACK HATS	My mum might not be able to come because she has my sister to look after.
	We'd have to shift all the tables in here and make our nice kitchen a bit grubby.
	There shouldn't be too much to learn or we could forget the words.
	Where are we to get the music and the magic coach.
	We haven't got a fairy godmother.
BLUE HAT	Mmmm. There's a lot to think about. Green Hats on everyone and think of ways we could solve these problems.
GREEN HATS	My mummy could bring the baby and she can feed her so that she sleeps.
	We can make up a script and learn lines like the real actors.
	We can put on a CD when we are dancing.
	We've got that car thing; we could put glittery cloth over it to make a fairy coach.
	Emily's got long fair hair. She could be the fairy godmother.
BLUE HATS	So we have to think about the play and who wants to play the parts and then there's all the other things like making tickets. What else would we need to do? Put your Green Hats on.
GREEN HATS	Make posters: Get more things for the dressing up box. We could use the maracas when the bad sisters come in.
	We need to make tickets. John's best at cutting out.
	How many people will come? Will they sit on our chairs?
	What will Mr Alex (the janitor) say if the room gets messy?
	We could bake cakes and have juice at the interval.

This interaction took place over three days for after the children gave their initial responses they had to go home and find out if their parents would like to come to the show and what day would be best. The practitioner 'Blue Hat' recapped each day and alerted the children to what would be happening at the next session. This gave them time to prepare. At each change of hat, the Blue Hat reminded the children what each hat signified: 'When you put on your Yellow Hats everyone has to think of happy things'.

Although using the six hats had been built up gradually with stories, some of the children were flustered and changing hats really interrupted their thoughts. But many children coped well especially the gifted and talented children. Using the strategy helped the plan to be organised and, most important of all, the children had ownership of the plot.

The script

With help from the older 11-year-old children the script was produced. They explained that the children could peak their parts or mime them. The children who did not wish to have a part formed a 'choir' and spoke together to support the actors

CINDERELLA:	I am Cinderella and I'm very, very sad.
EVERYONE:	She has a new stepmother and she's mad, mad mad!
CINDERELLA:	I have two ugly sisters, their names are Pol and Fay.
EVERYONE:	And when you have to look at them you want to run away!

EVERYONE:	Let's all help Cinderella to go to the Ball.
BUTTONS:	But what's she going to wear? She has nothing at all!
FAIRY GODMOTHER:	What does she need? A dress I think,
	Silk and net in a lovely pink.
	And dainty shoes, perhaps of glass?
	Then we'll see what comes to pass!
EVERYONE:	What a lot of joy the fairy godmother brings
	We were all so sad, but we're ready now to sing
	So everyone keep smiling, as happy as can be
	We're all ready for some jollity.
BUTTONS:	But who is that approaching? It's three old hags.
	They're telling Cinderella that she has only rags
EVERYONE:	Don't tell them our secret of the one who'll save the day
	With her wand she'll make our dreams come true
	And keep these hags away.
EVERYONE:	Hurrah for Cinderella, she's going to the ball
	She'll have a really magic time
	Who knows what might befall?
	But when she hears the clock strike twelve
	Homeward she must go,
	Or her pretty dress will disappear.
	Oh NO, Oh NO, Oh NO!
NARRATOR:	Cinderella's sitting sighing
(back at home in the kitchen)	When a knock comes to the door,
	In comes a prince, a stranger
	He's not been here before
PRINCE CHARMING	Can you fit this pretty shoe?
	The handsome prince enquires?
	And Cinderella slips it on
	Every one admires! Ah, ah, it's ON!
EVERYONE:	So there is a wedding
	With many, many guests
	The fairy godmother comes along
	At Cinderella's request.
	The bells ring out
	The sun shines bright
	And guess what happens now?
	The step mum and the sisters come,
	Join in and take their bow.
	What a happy story
	What a lovely tale we've told
	So sing a song along with us
	Don't stay out in the cold.
	For we have had a lovely time
	Making dreams come true
	And if you wish just hard enough
	They could come true for you!

EYFS goals: interact with others negotiating plans and taking turns in conversation.
SCE goals: Link and apply new learning in different situations.

Children composing and acting stories

Vivian Gussin Paley's work on children acting out their own small stories is intriguing.

Vivian begins with a group of children in a stage-shaped space (outlined by tape) and she explains that she is going to tell them a story a little boy in America wrote just for them, and then if they wish, they can act it out. She tells them the child's name, Ben, keeping the episode personal and meaningful and she reads the story from a notebook where Ben's name is at the top of the page. Ben's story is short and simple.

> A butterfly flew into the garden. It landed on a rock. Then it flew over some flowers and a house into the sky.

The children looked relieved that the story was like this. They immediately realised they could make up a story too. But before that happened, the children were asked if they would like to act out Ben's story. Each child was invited to have a turn and most volunteered to be the butterfly, the rock, the flowers and the house.

The next thing Vivian asked was, 'Would anyone like to tell me their story?' And before they did, she added their name to the book in her hand. This turned out to be very important to the children for when they went back to school and the teacher tried to replicate the experience, one child who had never spoken out in front of his friends before announced that he would like to tell his story. When the teacher asked him to begin, he demurred, 'Not yet, I can't, because you haven't written my name in your notebook!'

The important thing was that the stories belonged to the children and the atmosphere was so positive because of the respect with which the stories were received. And when the other children acted their stories out, the authors were so proud. This was a huge lesson in promoting a positive self-esteem.

So - teachers put on your Green Hats and think up some simple stories like this and envisage how the children could act them out. But only make your suggestions if none are forthcoming from the children. Gifted and talented children are likely to have many suggestions to lead the others but with children you never know!!

EYFS goals: enjoy listening to spoken language: explore and experiment with words and texts.
SCE goals: develop self-respect; achieve success in different arenas.

For 11-year-olds: Researching Edinburgh (but it could be anywhere!)

One school carried out an enterprising project in Edinburgh. The group of 'able children' in Primary 7 did an investigation into key tourist attractions. They compiled interview schedules in school and then visited the different venues.

1) Interviewing the organiser of the tourist buses

The children discovered how many buses were used; the routes they took; how many visitors came and what nationalities they were; what the visitors particularly wanted to see and how the company dealt with simultaneous translation of different languages. They also found out about the training necessary to be a guide.

2) Visit to a tartan shop and bagpipe maker

The children found out how bagpipes were made and about the demand from overseas and at home. They learned about the different tartans and clans and the correct way to wear a kilt both for day and evening wear. They discovered the cost of acquiring the whole outfit. They learned that other countries had pipes too and noted the differences in construction. And of course they tried to play the pipes!

3) Visit to the Museum of Childhood

The children found out how Scottish children lived long ago and about the toys and schooling that was so different to their own. They found how the artefacts had been accumulated. Seeing penny-farthing bikes and dolls houses from rich homes made their history lessons so meaningful.

4) Princes Street Gardens with its floral clock

The children met the gardeners and horticulturalists and found out about the planting schedule and how this was timed so that colourful displays would be ready for principal events. They were fascinated by the planting of the floral clock, a key visitor attraction.

The point of this was that the project was much more than a series of visits. The children had to prepare interview schedules and debate and discuss what questions would provide the richest answers. They had to make a schedule of visits when people were free to have them. They had to know who was going to ask what and who was going to thank the interviewees. This was filmed as an opportunity for enrichment and enhancement for able children. The venture in Edinburgh could be replicated in other environments.

I hope your children enjoy these activities as much as the Scottish children did!

Chapter 5

The gifted child with learning differences

Asynchronous development (ASD)

In this context ASD stands for asynchronous development. It should not be confused with the ASD often used to mean autistic spectrum disorders, a range of difficulties that are part of autism.

There are many children who have a distinctly uneven profile of abilities and difficulties. One five-year-old whose first written piece of work at school read 'There is chaos in the business world' with each word spelt correctly – threw a tantrum and was inconsolable because another child hung his coat on her peg! Her intellectual and her social/emotional competences were clearly mismatched! This asynchronous development (ASD), which can be mild to severe, is even more apparent and debilitating when the child has a learning difference that is not recognised by the teacher or understood by the other children in the class. Then the child can be bewildered and dismayed by questions such as, 'How can a clever child like you not do … or cope with?' This is compounded by a generally held but mistaken belief that the intellectually gifted child can use this ability to compensate for difficulties in the motor, social or emotional aspects of their development.

Graves (2004) paints a telling picture. He explains:

> I often see these children in the context of a beautiful piece of music which needs the sounds of the individual instruments (abilities and disabilities) adjusted by a stereo receiver. You know, the ones marked min. and max. and bass and treble for balance.

He explains that some children have instruments that work with ease and others with difficulty or even not at all. He ponders how having the ability to adjust the levers might give more balance to the child's development. Many children's, parents' and teachers' lives would be so enhanced if only this was possible. Rios (2000) calls this unequal development 'living with contradictions'.

It is not surprising that parents and practitioners can be confused or challenged by such discrepancies. They wonder how to provide the most beneficial learning opportunities for their children. Neihart (2003) advises that the most effective interventions always 'focus on the unique strengths' and she advises parents and practitioners to concentrate on 'developing the talent, while trying to support the disability'. In so doing, they will reassure the children that their talents have been recognised and valued. Keeping the disability in proportion will not compound the children's difficulties by impacting negatively on their self-esteem. 'Supporting the disability' can be accomplished by devising a plan of action with the children setting out steps that promise progress. A head teacher shares her thoughts. She explains:

> Over and over again I find that children will accept that a difficulty exists if a plan of action to reduce it is ready to guide their efforts. They have to see plans on paper rather than having vague promises that might in their eyes, not materialise. Anyway, written plans can act as checklists and they save remembering schedules – things these children find difficult to do.

Gifted and talented children have advantages in that they can do other things well, but this doesn't make having a disability easy. In fact both the children and their parents can be less accepting than children with a poor level of ability right across the board. They can be less patient and of course stress adds to the problem. If they have researched the subject then they may be distressed by realising that the disability isn't going to go away. At first the children may refuse to try compensatory strategies 'because everyone will think I'm stupid' (Nathan, aged 10) but after a while they come to accept that they need a sloping board for writing or a private space to cut out distracters or different timetables to keep them on track.

> The older children can even have simplified maps of the school layout or the walk home to help them be independent. After a bit they see how these visual aids really work and accept the support. Often the parents will say how well they work and become less emotional. Then the children don't feel they have let the parents down. But this doesn't happen overnight. There are no quick fixes. Everyone has to learn to be patient, I'm afraid!
>
> (Headteacher: Secondary School)

But what are these strengths and disabilities? (For a full explanation of each difficulty, see Macintyre 2005.)

In this brief account dyspraxia comes first, because poor movement competence is at the root of most, if not all additional need conditions.

Gifted and talented children with dyspraxia/dysgraphia

The key movement competences – balance, coordination and control – will be problematic in all these children. They will be the ones who fall over thin air, who bump and barge and hurt themselves and others in the process and produce very untidy work. Almost inevitably, this causes other children and adults to be impatient and sometimes sarcastic or unkind. And because they are of above average intelligence, these children are often denied the support their condition requires. So their self-esteem plummets and some, albeit in the more extreme cases, can become convinced that they are no use at all.

How will dyspraxia (movement learning difficulties) or dysgraphia (handwriting difficulties) impact on the learning of gifted and talented children and on their self-esteem? It is not difficult to imagine the confusion and frustration of such able children who have imaginative stories to tell or solutions to problems in their minds possibly before anyone else, yet they are unable to scribe their thoughts on paper. And if, in addition, they have the poor short-term memory difficulties associated with the 'dys' conditions (dyspraxia, dyslexia, dysgraphia and dyscalculia), then unrecorded ideas and innovative suggestions are very likely to be lost.

Lewis who is 8 explains:

> Having dyspraxia is like trying to light a fire with boxing gloves on and you can't take them off. It's like walking in treacle. I can't use escalators or run to keep up with the others. I don't get out of puff, my legs just won't move fast enough. I hate PE because I've just struggled to get dressed then the teacher makes me take my clothes off again. By the time I've done that I have to put them back on! Everyone laughs at me. My Mum says 'enough is enough' so I'm not going to go to that school any more. I wish everyone could have dyspraxia for a week then they would know how it feels. I'm a whiz on the computer though so I'll do my lessons at home now. What a huge relief!

Some children like Lewis with poor muscle tone in both his arms and legs can be severely disabled by dyspraxia, while others are much less affected. But as there are no outward signs, i.e. till the children move to complete a task, then it comes under the heading, 'a hidden handicap'. The earlier the condition is recognised, the sooner exercises to build up myelin (see Chapter 2) can be put in place and classroom strategies can be agreed, with the parents and children discussing what would be best.

Handwriting ability

So often, especially in the early years, 'neat work' equates with 'good work'. Is this because most very young children do not give enough content to stimulate other kinds of comment? So children with dyspraxia/dysgraphia, even if they have produced the most complex story or the most interesting and innovative solution to a problem may not receive the praise the work merits. If teachers only consider the appearance of the work the children may be told to 'write it out again'. And so distress is compounded by the teacher who, in the child's eyes, 'knows best'. One very articulate ten-year-old boy with dyspraxia explained his difficulty. 'I can see the writing in my head', he explained, 'I know what I want to do, but when it comes down to my hand it goes all wrong somehow'. His hands lacked the control to scribe the intricate patterns needed to produce the pictures he saw. This could be caused be hypotonia (poor muscle tone in the fingers, arms and shoulders) and strengthening work, given as soon as possible, should ideally be overseen by physiotherapists/occupational therapists. If these experts are not available, then working with clay, popping bubble paper, catching and throwing a ball can help as well as the pre-writing activities such as making big circles and crosses on large pieces of paper. However practitioners need to observe the children carefully to check that poor compensatory grips and postures don't become habitual. They also must check that the children are well balanced in their chairs when they attempt to write and that seats and desks are at the correct height (at elbow height when the child is seated).

When children with these control problems, as opposed to conceptual problems (not knowing what to write), are required to complete a writing task, it can mean cramped fingers, hunched shoulders and rising levels of frustration and bewilderment. Expert help is required to check whether these difficulties are caused by retained primitive reflexes. If they are, a programme of activities devised by Sally Goddard-Blythe can help (Goddard-Blythe 2005).

But what can be done in the setting?

Following Neihart's advice, it is essential to find another way to allow children to record their thoughts so that their strengths are recognised.

Audio equipment is needed for this to happen. This also allows the children to work at their own pace and ensures a level of independence. But it is difficult for teachers to find time to listen to tapes and quickly make suggestions for improvements. Another strategy would be to involve the children in more discussions and have the teacher or a child designated as 'recorder,' make a note of the ideas that are suggested. Some children who have dyspraxia, particularly those who find crossing the midline of the body difficult, find it much easier to use computers, because in that activity each hand works on its own side of the body. There is no need to cross the midline. And of course computing has the benefit of being seen as a valuable skill. Other children can be quite envious especially when the gifted and talented children can produce work that matches their abilities! This removes stress, encourages a much more positive attitude and allows the children's talent to flow. And with the influx of technology, perhaps the insistence that all children handwrite their work needs to be questioned anyway.

Of course dyspraxia affects much more than the ability to write, although often parents don't register their concern until this difficulty impacts on their child's progress across the curriculum. Cutting out, colouring in, using a knife and fork, being able to articulate clearly, even getting to the toilet in time; these competences, so often taken for granted, are all governed by muscles that may lack tone and affect control in children with 'dys' conditions. At home, difficulties in getting dressed either because of remembering what goes on first (planning, organising and sequencing difficulties), or because of the intricate fine motor skill required to tie laces or do up zips may first alert parents that something is not quite right, but often in the busyness of the day they will do these tasks for the children and so their difficulties are hidden from view.

Parents and practitioners have to remember that poor muscle tone may affect the internal muscles as well as those more easily seen. So poor bladder control, eyes that do not work together to give a clear picture or backs that simply won't allow children to sit or stand up straight are all possible parts

Figure 5.1 Liam is developing his sensory integration through listening and speaking into a recorder

of the conditions. And of course, although the children's work will certainly be affected, their innate intelligence is intact. These are specific learning difficulties (SLDs). This term indicates that one aspect of the child's development is significantly lower than what could have been anticipated from any IQ score. So gifted and talented children can have conditions like these. Yet in the playground these children are often called 'thick' and if they are not given a label to explain their difficulties to the other professionals and to the children in their class, they may come to believe it themselves. Many children are left bitter by such false accusations. Unfortunately parents are still finding that their doctors are unsure and often unwilling to make a diagnosis. This may be because there are no tests and no definite cut-off scores to differentiate between those who have and those who do not have the condition. This is done by 'expert eyes' and practitioners such as physiotherapists having a sound knowledge of difficulties. So making a diagnosis without the opportunity to make extended observations over time is very difficult.

What can be done in the setting?

If parents and practitioners who have many more opportunities to observe the children suspect there are difficulties that should be confirmed as a condition, they have to get expert help so that the most appropriate support is put in place. Taking video footage as evidence of their concerns is vitally important. This means that misunderstandings between practitioners and physiotherapists can be avoided. These can arise because it is so difficult to describe movements in words. It is so important that communications are accurate, for children must be helped before their self-esteem suffers.

A vitally important clue: teach the children to crawl, for 80 per cent of children with handwriting difficulties will not have crawled!

It is essential to assess every child's ability to balance and to crawl using cross lateral coordination, because these activities set up a template in the child's brain and this eases further learning. In a crawling position the children are near the ground; they feel safe and with explanations or demonstrations, most will learn to lift one arm or leg in turn to move forward. (Practitioners should be sure they check cross lateral co-ordination, i.e. that the children are using alternate hands and knees, not moving limbs on the same side!) Then, once they can crawl, they can go in and out of table legs, up inclines and up stairs for the hands and knees climbing pattern is the same as the crawling one, over benches, in line with a partner or wherever they want to go. They can even blow balloons along the ground or dribble a ball in and out of skittles as they crawl. Perseverance in achieving this pattern and daily repetitions till the pattern is fully internalised will pay rich dividends. Even in Key Stage 2 crawling games like this can rewrite faulty early movement patterns. It is never too late to improve.

Ensure the children have hand and foot dominance

Often children who fumble and mistime actions do so because they have a poor sense of hand or foot dominance. This develops as the children mature. Three-year-olds will happily draw using either hand and kick a ball with either foot. But as they approach school age it is important that they recognise a preference, i.e. which hand or foot gives the best results. Otherwise confusion and fumbling or stumbling can be the result. Sometimes parents will claim that their child is ambidextrous but that is only true in a few cases. Much more likely is the fact that the child has not achieved hand and foot dominance.

What can be done in the setting?

Practitioners can help the children to decide which hand or foot gives the best results by setting up small games that include some scoring. The little girl in the picture was asked to crawl from the corner, to pick up a beanbag and throw it into the pail. She tried, sometimes using one hand and sometimes the other. So the question to make her think about success was, 'Which hand gets most beanbags in the pail?' Other similar games were tried, e.g. getting her to catch a ping-pong ball that rolled down an inclined piece of cardboard and asking, 'Which hand was best at catching the ball?' or kicking a stationary ball into a goalmouth and asking, 'Which foot scored the most goals!' So the child decided on the 'best hand/foot to use' and after that the practitioners gently reminded her of her choice when she appeared undecided or confused.

Planning and organising

Children with dyspraxia and those with dyslexia and all the other conditions are likely to have planning and organisational problems. 'It is very difficult to find the "pure" child' (Kirby 1999) and poor organisation, planning and sequencing will almost certainly be a co-occurring difficulty across

Figure 5.2 Lila is showing whether she has developed hand dominance

Figure 5.3 The children gather fallen leaves, fill the pit and enjoy playing in their homemade leaf pool

the various syndromes (Macintyre and Deponio 2003). So the wonderful work these children can produce may be left at home, or be lost ,or be messed up by rubbing out, causing annoyance and frustration to parents and teachers as well as the children themselves.

What can be done in the setting

Planning, sequencing and organising problems go hand-in-hand with poor short-term memories, so having visual aids and timetables for every part of the day, from putting clothes on in the correct order to making the routine of the school day visual can reduce stress and let the children concentrate on areas where their gifts and talents will shine through.

Helping sequencing is also important. So when telling stories, recaps focusing on the order of events – asking 'what happened first and what came next?' – can be useful aids in helping planning and organising.

Gifted and talented children with dyslexia

Fortunately there has been a great deal of research into dyslexia and usually, although not always, children's difficulties (mainly reading and spelling but with linked problems with planning, organising and sequencing, rhythm and poor short-term memory and motor skills) are readily recognised and strategies to match the profile of difficulties each child has, are put in place. However both dyspraxia and dyslexia are specific learning difficulties, meaning that the children's intellectual level may be very high and the most able children may use rote-learning strategies to cloak their difficulties. So these may not be recognised till later when the critical learning time is past. Often this concerns difficulty in recognising sounds or phonics. Carrying out research for her PhD thesis, 'Otitis media – a new diagnosis for dyslexia?' Lindsay Peer, at that time Director of the Dyslexia Institute found that many children had a hearing difficulty at the critical time for learning the sounds of their mother tongue. While they were not deaf and so responded normally to instructions, they were unable to differentiate between sounds such as 'p', 'b', and 'd'. This affected both reading and spelling for this skill often requires children to sound out the words in their head before transferring what they hear to paper. It is essential that hearing discrimination problems are identified early; else overlearning and rote learning have to compensate for not hearing sounds distinctly. Practitioners should try to check this perhaps by playing games where children repeat sounds. Some visual learners of course see patterns rather than hearing the sounds so their problems lie in processing the information they have received.

It is so interesting to note that in the Far East where the children read with pictograms, rather than with letters (which look alike and may even move on the page if Mears-Irlen Syndrome is present), dyslexia barely exists. Most children with dyslexia will think in pictures; they will be right-brain dominant and, as such, will be more creative and spatially aware than their left-brain dominant peers. They are usually able to visualise 3D models and may be able to assemble toys or tables, even computers, without being able to read the instructions. Unfortunately there are concepts and ideas that do not readily come in picture form and therein lies the problems that children with dyslexia face.

In the nursery, many steps are taken to make the curriculum visual. While this is splendid it can confuse! One little boy was convinced his name was 'tractor'. Well that was the picture beside his coat, wasn't it? There is so little time for practitioners to explain!

Slow speech development

Despite being very bright, children can have slow speech development and when they do speak they tend to get words muddled, e.g. cubumber, weletison. At home some parents may unwittingly compound the difficulty by 'having fun' mimicking the child's language. But it is so important that children learn to articulate accurately and so speak with confidence before they begin to attempt to read. Delay may be caused by poor hearing or listening skills and these should be checked as early as possible.

What can be done in the setting?

Practitioners are advised by the Lothian Speech and Language Unit to:

- Give the children choices so that they have to say something: 'Would you like milk or water?' rather than 'Would you like a drink?' a question that could be answered by a nod or a shake of the head.
- Use stories or rhymes with repetitive lines, for example 'The Gingerbread Man' or 'The Little Red Hen' so that the child knows when and how to join in. Practitioners should pause to allow the child to respond.
- If the child volunteers a word, for example 'car' expand this 'Oh yes that's a big car. Is it the same as Daddy's?' This is because children learn language from hearing it.
- Avoid correcting children's speech. Encourage them to communicate even if they don't do so 'properly'. A gentle repetition of a 'faulty' word in a sentence is more effective that a one-word repetition because that suggests the child's contribution was awry. Competence will come when confidence develops.

Poor naming skills

Sometimes even gifted children with dyslexia forget the names of their friends, their teachers and take a surprisingly long time to get to grips with naming colours. These are naming abilities led by the left-hand side of the brain. The left side is often smaller in children with dyslexia. Could this be down to under usage in the earliest years?

A poor sense of rhythm

Many children with dyslexia avoid rhythmical activities; little ones do not enjoy nursery rhymes or clapping games. Yet language is rhythmical and the children's reading will be eased and made more flowing if they can listen to and replicate rhythmical phrases. Many jingles emphasising rhythm in a fun activities can be found in *Jingle Time* (Macintyre 2003). Rhymes such as 'incy wincy spider' and old fashioned circle games such as The Hokey Kokey, all help.

Poor speed of processing

This links with children's poor organisation because if they cannot keep up with one instruction, then subsequent ones are lost. Many adults will remember the horror of mental arithmetic tests when delay in finding the answer to one question meant not hearing the next!

What can be done in the setting?

- First of all ensure that any background noise (humming radiators, chatting colleagues or children, outside noises) is minimised because many children cannot cut out distracters in the environment and this makes listening even harder.
- Try to face the children and speak directly to them. So often practitioners have to multitask and they speak to children while looking out over their heads to monitor others.
- Praise good listening and good paying attention rather than waiting for a finished piece of work.
- Give one instruction at a time and rephrase rather than repeat if the first instruction has not been followed. Only when one instruction is followed competently should a second be added.

The gifted child with dyscalculia or mathematical dyslexia

Some children who have sequencing problems and memory difficulties find that these can affect their number sense too. As a result they have difficulty getting to grips with mathematical concepts and mathematical language.

What can be done in the setting?

- Give children the opportunity to feel words e.g. in the hall, stand 'opposite' a partner; go 'through' his legs (developing spatial awareness); stand 'behind' the table; bring me the biggest ball; squeeze between the wall and the desk and so on. (Practitioners remember to check that the children understand, not simply copy the child beside them.)
- Have lining-up games to explain concepts like bigger and smaller and tie these in with desk games that require the child to understand these concepts. 'Snakes and ladders 'can help children understand directions (the ladders slope diagonally) in a fun environment.
- Always have concrete objects so that the child can hold them, feel the weight, and/or understand whether they can change shape. This develops pictures in the child's mind and helps later abstract thinking.
- Tessellation activities can help the older children.

Gifted and talented children with ADD/ADHD (attention deficit disorder and attention deficit hyperactivity disorder)

The attention deficit disorders are genetic, neurobiological difficulties subject to much mis-understanding. Some people mistakenly say that the hyperactive group of children are badly behaved when neurological problems mean they cannot resist the urge to move or call out. In 2007 some doctors even deny that such conditions exist. Yet they can be profoundly disabling, disrupting family life, often to an intolerable degree. Nutritional supplements containing fatty acids and medications that stimulate the flow of dopamine, one of the neurotransmitters in the brain can help many children. However, any medication must be monitored carefully under medical supervision to ensure that possible side effects are controlled.

The difficulties which children with the attention deficit disorders face centre around not being able to focus on activities. The children have to be intrigued, else their attention quickly wanders. Children with ADD, and these are predominantly girls, tend to daydream and withdraw from the learning that is happening in the classroom. Children with the hyperactivity element (ADHD), and these are usually boys, will quickly change focus and find something else to do. They find it difficult to stay in their seats and this causes disruption in the classroom. Teachers and parents, as well as the children themselves, often despair.

Yet many children with these difficulties *can focus* for significant periods of time if they are sufficiently enthralled by the task in hand. When they are less interested however, they are easily distracted, and they feel compelled to move to discover something else out there that appeals more than completing what they have been asked to do. Their bodies have to catch up with their minds and the most able children, even when they are aware of the effect this is having on their work and, perhaps even more importantly on their peers attitude to them, can't resist the impulse to move. Constantly being told off for something they can't help means they become frustrated and possibly aggressive. But when the children concentrate hard to stay still, they may find that the effort needed to do so detracts from their ability to do well. Gifted chess players with ADHD have been beaten by less competent opponents because their efforts to be quiet and still detracts from the concentration needed to play the game.

What can be done in the setting?

Very often gifted children with ADHD can recognise their anxieties and urges to move building up and teachers, recognising that this is a neurobiological condition, not poor behaviour have to listen to the children and allow them to move beyond the confines of the classroom. Many children will be able to explain the kinds of experiences that they find calming or they may prefer movement activities that rid their bodies of surplus energy. If they can be allowed to follow their preferences, they are less likely to distract their peers and cause resentment in class or in the playground where recriminations can lead to escalating aggressive behaviour.

There have been strategies that in practice have not proved to be helpful, especially to gifted and talented children. Suggestions to give the children shorter pieces of work so that they have the satisfaction of completing something have not worked. This is because the children's motivation depends on their dealing with complex challenging issues that need time and patience to solve. So simplifying and shortening tasks is not the answer. They enjoy tasks that depend on them finding resources, new materials or 'moving out of one space' activities, allow them to confront new challenges.

Unfortunately these children are often labelled as being difficult to handle and other children can set them off, then retreat from the ensuing disturbance. Teachers have to understand the condition, else blame can be unfairly added to the stress these children live with every day. Teachers are asked to identify triggers by noting what caused the incident that caused a disturbance, record who was present and the length of time the incident lasted. In this way 'evidence' can be shared with experts in the field and the most appropriate plans to support the children can be put in place.

Teachers are also asked to redefine the way they think and talk about these children. Advice given from the Learning Assessment and Neurocare Centre says:

> Instead of saying children are 'out of their seats too much', say they are lively and enthusiastic. Think of them as being energetic learners and recognise that they do best with individual programmes of study and one-to-one interaction.

They also suggest the following strategies,

- Take the age of a child with ADHD and subtract 30 per cent to get their true behavioural and emotional age;
- Don't let MBUs (minor behavioural upsets) get you down;
- Control less – don't 'confront' unnecessarily;
- Drop into the way they learn – communicate – visually, kinaesthetically, or in auditory mode;
- Use timetables, routines and try not to change order of activities (avoid disruptions);
- Allow the children to use cmoputers because then 'they exhibit abilities that they don't typically demonstrate in other settings and tasks' (Shaw 2006).

No one is suggesting that following this advice is easy, but these children are crying out for understanding and support. ADHD has been rated as having the same level of effect as depression and/or Tourette's syndrome. Eighty per cent of specialists claim that ADHD has the most or second most negative impact on a child's development (ADDiSS 2004). Gifted and talented or not, these children need support and understanding if they are to fulfil the potential they undoubtedly have.

Gifted and talented children with Asperger's syndrome

Children with intellectual gifts may also have Asperger's syndrome, which is the condition often called 'the high functioning end of the autistic spectrum'. Despite being intellectually very able, these children have the poor social communication and the lack of imagination that are key symptoms of autism. Being bright, the children recognise their problems but cannot work out how to overcome them. This often leads to sadness and depression.

Giftedness in Asperger's syndrome is often of a kind that labels the children 'mono savants'. This means that they are highly competent in a particular sphere but very often cannot transfer that learning apply it in another, even linked field. George Weiner, often known as 'Calendar Man', can immediately tell which day of the week birthdays fall on in any year and he has memorised hundreds of books. Yet this skill doesn't transfer to being able to apply the gift in another sphere. The lack of imagination that is part of Asperger's syndrome may prevent mono savants seeing possibilities or they may have an overriding obsession to accrue more lists or timetables or whatever gives them satisfaction. They lack the desire as well as the competence to find how their data could be used effectively in another situation.

Certainly the social isolation that generally surrounds these children is a huge handicap to sharing ideas and putting heads together to peruse different outcomes, but identifying a second child who shares the same interests and allowing them to focus on the activity rather than the togetherness may be a start. If communication is artificially forced, children with Asperger's syndrome are likely to be confused by not understanding the reactions of others to their overtures and of course the inability to read non-verbal cues may mean that their attempts to foster communication are inappropriate, causing them huge distress.

But of course the gift that the child with Asperger's syndrome has must be nourished or how else are the children to make their way in the world? The obsessive interest can lead to successful employment even if it is rather solitary. The person who enjoys focusing and derives much satisfaction from being allowed to follow one path may not see this as a disadvantage. There are many gifted people who have used the commitment or obsession of their interest to do extraordinarily well. Their gifts have made them authors at a young age such as Luke Jackson, business entrepreneurs such as Temple Grandin, inventors such as Bill Gates and the greatest of all, Einstein.

Whenever children have difficulties, it is important to see the child's gifts first and any need as something that can be helped. Else how is self-esteem to be enhanced? And is that not the most important consideration of all? Graves (2004) revisiting his musical analogy asks,

> How poor would the world have been if people like Mozart (ADHD) had not had people in their lives to help them orchestrate their compositions?

What can be done in the setting?

Three ways of interacting with children with Asperger's syndrome/autism have been advised. They are:
1   ABA or applied behaviour analysis
2   PECS or picture exchange system
3   TEACHH

Both ABA and TEACHH depend on intensive one-to-one interaction. Every skill is broken down into meaningful parts and taught in a precise and systematic way. Depending on the child's level of impairment these skills may be life skills, the activities of daily living or they may be more aligned to what is taught in schools. Repetition and rewards for success are at the root of progress. The picture exchange system is most often used when autistic children have no spoken language and selecting pictures is the best way for them to make their needs known. However it can also be used with children who have sequencing and organisational problems. In these cases the pictures can tell the child what tasks he has to complete and the order in which they should be done. When he has finished one, he can put his picture into the 'finished tray', just as the other children do with their pieces of work.

A final word comes from Temple Grandin who, despite or perhaps even because of Asperger's syndrome is a highly successful business woman, asks,

> What would happen if you eliminated autism from the gene pool? You would have a bunch of people standing around, chatting and socialising and never getting anything done!

Food for thought indeed!

Aspects of development

Age	Play	Language	Movement
5 years	Can initiate or join in role play	Can follow a story without pictures. Can read simple words.	Can run and jump, ride a bike and zip a coat. Understands the rules of major games.
4 years	Understands pretence and develops fears of the unknown. Develops imaginative games, not always able to explain rules.	Knows colours and numbers. Can explain events, hopes and disappointments. Able to listen and focus.	Can climb and swing on large apparatus. Has a developed sense of safety outdoors. Can swim. Enjoys bunny jumps and balancing activities.
3 years	Enjoys group activities, e.g. baking a cake for someone's birthday. Understands turn taking.	Uses complex sentences. Understands directional words and simple comparisons e.g. big/small.	Can ride a trike and climb stairs. Climbs in and out of cars/ buses independently. Can catch a large ball.
2½ years	Develops altruism especially for family members. Understands emotional words, e.g. happy, sad.	Uses pronouns and past tenses adding 'ed' to form own version of past tense.	Uses a step-together pattern to climb stairs. Can walk some distance.
2 years	Beginning to play alongside a friend for a short time. (parallel play)	Rebels – says 'No'. Can form two word sentences but comprehension is far ahead of speech.	Can walk well but jumping is still difficult. Climbs on furniture (crawling pattern).
18 months	Sensorimotor play exploring the properties of objects (solitary play)	Has ten naming words. Points to make wishes known.	Can crawl at speed and walk but jumping is not developed. Balance is precarious!
1 year	Walks unsteadily, arms and step pattern wide to help balance.	Enjoys games e.g. peek-a-boo. Beginning to enjoy books and stories. Monosyllabic babbling.	Plays with toys giving them correct usage – simple pretend, e.g. feeding doll.
6–8 months	Can sit unsupported briefly Rolls over. Attempts to crawl.	Makes sounds and blows bubbles.	Reaching out for objects now. Changing objects from one hand to the other.
0–4 months	May be able to support head but weight of head makes this difficult. Strength developing head to toe and centre to periphery. Can lift head briefly in front lying.	Early communication: responds to voices. Can make needs known.	Plays with hands as first toy. Can hold object placed in hand but cannot let go – object drops.

Source: Macintyre 2007.

Cognitive development

Indicators of giftedness: (30 per cent more advanced)

- Alertness
- Heightened perceptual awareness
- Intensity of purpose
- Curiosity
- Task commitment
- Extended concentration span
- Advanced play behaviour
- Exceptional memory
- Fast pace of learning
- Asks probing questions
- Early interest in books and print
- Early reading
- Exceptional mathematical ability
- Creative/imaginative
- Shows attention to detail: follows complex instructions
- Sense of humour: creates own puns and analogies
- Able to understand complex concepts

Contrasting milestones

	Normal (months)	30% advanced
Physical development		
Lifts chin while lying on front	1	0.7
Rolls over	3	2.1
Sits with support	4	2.8
Sits alone	7	4.9
Stands with help	8	5.6
Stands alone securely	11	7.7
Walks alone	12.5	8.7
Creeps up stairs	15	10.5
Walks up stairs	18	12.6
Runs well	24	16.8
Jumps – two feet off ground	30	21.0
Rides tricycle using pedals	36	25.2
Throws ball	48	33.6
Skips – alternate feet	60	42.0
Fine motor development		
Plays with rattle	3	2.1
Holds object between finger and thumb	9	6.3
Scribbles spontaneously	13	9.1

Draws person with two body parts	48	33.6
Draws recognisable person with body	60	42.
Draws person with neck, hands and clothes	72	50.4
Language development		
Vocalises two different sounds	2.3	1.6
Vocalises four different syllables	7	4.9
Says first word	7.9	5.5
Responds to name	9	6.3
Babbles with intonation	12	8.4
Imitates words	12.5	8.7
Vocabulary of 4–6 words	15	10.5
Names an object	17.8	12.5
Vocabulary of 10 words	18	12.6
Vocabulary of 20 words	21	14.7
Combines several words spontaneously	21	14.7
Uses simple sentences	24	16.8
Uses personal pronouns	24	16.8

Source: Hall and Skinner (1980).

Goals from Scotland's *A Curriculum for Excellence* (2007)

The report *A Curriculum for Excellence*, has a unified set of purposes for the early years, primary and secondary school to enable young people to become:

Successful learners

with

- enthusiasm and motivation for learning
- determination to reach high standards of achievement
- openness to new thinking and ideas

and able to

- use literacy, communication and numeracy skills
- use technology for learning
- think creatively and independently
- learn independently and as part of a group
- make reasoned evaluations
- link and apply different kinds of learning in new situations.

Responsible citizens

with

- respect for others
- commitment to participate responsibly in political, economic, social and cultural life

and able to

- develop knowledge and understanding of the world and Scotland's place in it
- understand different beliefs and cultures
- make informed choices and decisions
- evaluate environmental, scientific and technological issues
- develop informed ethical views of complex issues.

Confident individuals

with

- self-respect
- a sense of physical mental and emotional wellbeing
- secure values and beliefs
- ambition

and able to

- relate to others and manage themselves
- pursue a healthy and active lifestyle
- be self-aware
- develop and communicate their own beliefs and a view of the world
- live as independently as they can
- assess risk and make informed decisions
- achieve success in different areas of activity.

Effective contributors
with

- an enterprising attitude
- resilience
- self-reliance

and able to

- communicate in different ways and in different settings
- work in partnership and in teams
- take the initiative and lead
- apply critical thinking in new contexts
- create and develop
- solve problems.

Glossary

amygdala an almond shaped structure involved in the development of emotional intelligence; it detects fear-inducing events and stores emotional memories.

autism an inherited condition characterised by a lack of social awareness, imagination or ability to interpret non-verbal communication; Asperger's syndrome holds the same characteristics but the children are intellectually much brighter.

axons the long bundles of nerve fibres wiring the nervous system; each neuron has one axon that connects with thousands of others; each axon should be covered by myelin.

balance a key competence comes from the vestibular sense and either dynamic (moving) or static balance (stillness) operates constantly to provide spatial awareness.

brainstem the part of the brain connecting the two cerebral hemispheres to the spinal cord; it regulates breathing, blood pressure and heartbeat and so is essential to survival.

central nervous system the brain, spinal cord and optic nerves are all part of the CNS; it is connected to the peripheral nervous system which is made up of afferent nerves that carry sensory impulses from all parts of the body to the brain and efferent nerves that take motor impulses to the muscles initiating action.

cerebellum a structure which lies above the brainstem and has two hemispheres like the cortex; it doesn't initiate anything, but receives and controls all the motor and sensory impulses and directs them to the correct place for analysis.

cerebrospinal fluid a watery fluid that surrounds the brain and spinal cord; it is derived from the bloodstream and is filtered by a membrane in the ventricles in the brain.

cerebrum the main part of the brain divided into two hemispheres connected by the corpus collosum; both hemispheres are involved in most activities although each has a separate key function.

cognition the human features of the brain including speech and comprehension, memory, logical thinking and problem solving, calculation and visual and auditory perception.

coordination the organisation of muscle groups to provide movement; cross-lateral coordination should be demonstrated in crawling at eight months or so; hand–eye coordination and foot–eye coordination are also important for motor control.

corpus collosum a thick band of fibrous tissue that allows transmission of impulses between the two cerebral hemispheres; it is larger in gifted children; smaller in boys.

cortex the outer layer of the cerebrum where thinking occurs; it houses a band of neurons about 4mm thick.

dendrite the thin strand of the neuron that has receptors to receive messages which are then passed into the nucleus.

gene a uniquely coded segment of DNA that affects one or more specific body processes or developments.

genotype the pattern of characteristics and developmental sequences mapped in the genes of any specific individual; it will be modified by individual experience into the phenotype.

glial cells the cells that support the neurons and make myelin; they protect the neurons and carry away waste matter e.g. dead neuronal tissue.

grey matter the name for the cortex where neurons are concentrated.

hemisphere half of the cortex which is then subdivided into four regions; frontal (behind the forehead); temporal (behind the temples) parietal (at the top of the head) and occipital (right at the back).

hippocampus part of the temporal lobe behind the amygdala associated with memory and learning; it regulates hormones in the body and helps maintain temperature.

memory there are different types of memory including: procedural memory (that retains information about how to do skills such as riding a bike); episodic memory (allowing recall from times past), working, short-term memory (which retains information for a short time before it is discarded or passed to the long-term store).

myelin the fatty sheath that covers and protects the axon; myelin increases the speed at which messages can be sent; in some children it is very slow to build and activity is the key stimulant.

neurons the individual thinking cells that connect to other cells by their axons and synapses.

neurotransmitters chemicals stored near the end of the axon; when an electrical impulse reaches the synapse it releases neurotransmitters across the synapse; there are fifty different ones that control the transmission of stimuli across the synapse; these include dopamine, serotonin and adrenaline.

phenotype the expression of a particular set of genetic information in a specific environment.

proprioception awareness of position of the body in space during movement.

sensory cortex this area holds networks of neurons that process sensations from the different senses – pain, temperature, touch, balance (vestibular) vision, hearing proprioception and kinaesthesis.

synapse the gap connecting neurons to each other; one neuron may have 10,000 connections to other neurons.

white matter the myelinated neuronal fibres (axons) and supporting glial cells making up much of the nervous system.

Bibliography

ADDiSS (2004) Attention Deficit Hyperactivity Disorder Information Booklet, London: ADDiSS.

Barry, M. (2007) 'Labelling students, what purpose is served?', *Learn: Journal of the Irish Learning Support Agency*, 28.

Bee, H. (2004) *The Growing Child*, New York: HarperCollins College.

Bornstein, M.H. and Sigman M.D. (1986).Continuity in mental development from infancy', *Child Development*, 57: 251–74.

Caplan, N., Choy, M. and Whitmore J. (1992) 'Indochinese refugee families and academic achievement', *Scientific American*, 266, Feb., 18–24.

Carter, R. (2000) *Mapping the Mind*, London: Phoenix Books.

City of Edinburgh Council (2001) *A Framework for Gifted and Talented Pupils*, Edinburgh: City of Edinburgh Council

City of Edinburgh Council (2008) *A Curriculum for Excellence*, Edinburgh: City of Edinburgh Council.

DCSF (2005) The Standards Site. http://www.standards.dfes.gov.uk/giftedandtalented/.

De Bono, E. (1999) *Six Thinking Hats*, London: Penguin Books.

DfES (Department for Education and Skills)(2007) *Statutory Framework for The Early Years Foundation Stage: Setting the Standards for Learning, Development and Care for Children from Birth to Five*, Nottingham: DfES.

Eisenberg, N. (1992) *The Caring Child*, Cambridge, MA: Harvard University Press

Freeman, J. (1980) 'Research into Gifted Children', project funded by the Gulbenkein foundation and reported in R. Povey (ed.) *Educating the Gifted Child*, London: Harper and Row.

Gardner, H. (1983) *Frames of Mind: The Theory of Multiple Intelligences*, New York: Basic Books.

Gardner, H. (2006) *Five Minds for the Future*, Cambridge, MA: Harvard Business School Publishers.

Goddard, S. (1995) *A Teacher's Window into the Child's Mind*, Eugene, OR: Fern Ridge Press.

Goddard, S. (2002) *Reflexes, Learning and Behaviour*, Eugene, OR: Fern Ridge Press.

Goddard-Blythe, S. (2005) *The Well Balanced Child*, Stroud: Hawthorn Press.

Graves, L.S. (2004)'To be a gifted learner with learning challenges', *Learn: Journal of the Irish Learning Support Agency*, 26: 47–56.

Greenfield, P.M. (2007) 'Cognitive aspects of formal education', in D. Wagner and H. Stevenson (eds) *Cultural Perspectives on Child Development*, San Francisco, CA: Freeman.

Hall, E.G. and Skinner, N. (1980) *Identifying Gifted Preschoolers. Somewhere to Turn: Strategies for Parents of the Gifted and Talented Children*, New York: Teachers College Press

Hirsh J. (2007) Interview in 'Our Brilliant Brain' television series, London: Channel 4.

Hwang, P., Broberg, A. and Lamb, B. (1990) 'Swedish childcare research', in E. Melluish and P. Moss (eds) *Daycare for Young Children: International Perspectives*, London: Routledge.

Jackson, L. (2004) *Freaks, Geeks and Asperger Syndrome: A User's Guide to Adolescence*, London: Jessica Kingsley Publishers.

Kirby, A. (1999) *Dyspraxia: The Hidden Handicap*, London: David Fulton Publishers.

Lightfoot, L. (2005) 'New test "will find under-performing but gifted pupils', *Daily Telegraph*, 3 December. Available online http://www.telegraph.co.uk/news/main.jhtml?xml=/news/2005/12/03/ntests03.xml&sSheet=/news/2005/12/03/ixhome.html

Marland, S.P., Jnr. (1972) *Education of the Gifted and Talented*, Washington, DC: US Government Printing Office.

Macintyre, C. (2000) *Dyspraxia in the Early Years*, London: David Fulton Publishers.

Macintyre, C. (2003) *Jingle Time*, London: David Fulton Publishers.

Macintyre, C. (2005) *Identifying Additional Learning Needs: Listening to the Children*, London: Routledge.

Macintyre, C. (2007) *Understanding Children's Development in the Early Years: Questions Practitioners Often Ask*, London: Routledge.

Macintyre, C. (2008) Ongoing research. Parents' perspectives on their gifted and talented children.

Macintyre, C. and Deponio, P. (2003) *Assessing and Supporting Children with Specific Learning Difficulties: Looking Beyond the Label to Assess the Whole Child*, London: Routledge.

Meadows, S. (2002) *The Child as Thinker: The Development and Acquisition of Cognition in Childhood*, London: Routledge.

Melby, J.N. and Conger, R.D. (1996) 'Parental behaviours and children's performance: a longitudinal analysis' *Journal of Research on Adolescence*, 6: 113–37.

Melluish E.C. (1990) *Research on Daycare for Young Children in the UK: International Perspectives*, London: Routledge.

Moore, C. (2004) *George and Sam*, London: Viking Publications.

Naisbitt A.E. (2001) *Creating the Inclusive Classroom: Meeting the Needs of Gifted and Talented Children in the Mainstream Classroom*, Redcar: Cleveland Publications.

Neihart, M. (2003) 'Gifted children with attention deficit hyperactivity disorder', *ERIC EC Digest*, 649.

Paley, V.G. (2005) *A Child's Work: The Importance of Fantasy Play*, Chicago, IL: Chicago Press.

Parkhurst, J.T. and Asher, S.R. (1992) 'Peer rejection in middle school: subgoup differences in behaviour, loneliness and interpersonal concerns', *Educational Psychology*, 28(2): 231–41.

Peer, L. (2004) 'Otitis media: a new hypothesis in dyslexia?', paper presented at the BDA International Conference, University of Warwick, March.

Restak, R. (1991) *The Brain has a Mind of Its Own*, New York: Harmony Books.

Rios, M.V. (2000) 'Living with contradictions', in Kiesa Kay (ed.) *Uniquely Gifted: Identifying and Meeting the Needs of Exceptional Students*, Gilsum, NH: Avocus Publishing.

Scarr, S.(1992) 'Developmental theories and individual differences in IQ', *Child Development*, 63: 1–19.

Scottish Executive (2006) *The Child at the Centre*, Edinburgh: The Scottish Executive.

Shaw, R. (2006) *The Impact of Computer Mediated and Traditional Academic Tasks on the Performance and Behaviour of Children with ADHD*, Horsham: The Learning Assessment and Neurocare Centre.

Silverman, L.R. (1993) *A Developmental Model for Counselling the Gifted and Talented*, Denver, CO: Love Publishing Company.

Smith, P.K., Cowie, H. and Blades, M.(2002) *Understanding Children's Development*, 3rd edition, Oxford: Blackwell Publishers.

Sroufe, L.A. (2004) *Studying Lives Through Time: Personality and Development*, Washington, DC: American Psychological Association.

Sroufe, L.A., Eyeland, B. and Kreutzer, T. (1990) 'The fate of early experience following developmental change', *Child Development*, 61: 1363–73.

Thomas A. and Chess S. (1977) *Temperament and Development*, New York: Brunner/Mazel.

Torrance, E.P. (1972) 'Predictive validity of the Torrance tests of creative thinking', *Journal of Creative Behaviour*, 6: 236–52.

Trevarthen, C. (1977) 'Play for Tomorrow', Edinburgh: Edinburgh University Video Production.

Winkley, D. (2003) 'Grey matters: current neurological research and its implications for educators', http://www.keele.ac.uk/depts/ed/kisnet/interviews/winkley.htm.

Winkley, D. (2004) '"Grey matters": Current neurological research and its implications for educators', Summer paper, University of Keele.

Winner, L. (2007) Interview in 'Our Brilliant Brain'. television series, London: Channel 4.

Winston, R. (2004) *The Human Mind*, London: Bantam Books.

Index